PENGUIN CANADA

FROM FREE TRADE TO FORCED TRADE

Peter Urmetzer was educated at Carleton University
(BA, MA) and the University of British Columbia,
where he received his PhD in sociology and taught
for three years. He currently teaches at the Okanagan
University College in Kelowna and Vernon, British
Columbia. Mr. Urmetzer lectures on Canadian
society, research methods, and social inequality and
has had articles published in *Canadian Public Policy*,
BC Studies, and the *Canadian Journal of Political
Science* (all with Don Blake and Neil Guppy). His
research interests are economic globalization, political
economy, and the welfare state. He lives in Coldstream,
British Columbia.

FROM FREE TRADE
TO FORCED TRADE

Canada in the Global Economy

PETER URMETZER

PENGUIN
CANADA

PENGUIN CANADA

Published by the Penguin Group

Penguin Books, a division of Pearson Canada, 10 Alcorn Avenue, Toronto, Ontario,
    Canada M4V 3B2
Penguin Books Ltd, 80 Strand, London WC2R 0RL, England
Penguin Putnam Inc., 375 Hudson Street, New York, New York 10014, U.S.A.
Penguin Books Australia Ltd, 250 Camberwell Road, Camberwell, Victoria 3124, Australia
Penguin Books India (P) Ltd, 11, Community Centre, Panchsheel Park,
    New Delhi – 110 017, India
Penguin Books (NZ) Ltd, cnr Rosedale and Airborne Roads, Albany, Auckland 1310,
    New Zealand
Penguin Books (South Africa) (Pty) Ltd, 24 Sturdee Avenue, Rosebank 2196, South Africa

Penguin Books Ltd, Registered Offices: 80 Strand, London WC2R 0RL, England

First published 2003

10 9 8 7 6 5 4 3 2 1

Manufactured in Canada.

NATIONAL LIBRARY OF CANADA CATALOGUING IN PUBLICATION

Urmetzer, Peter, 1955–
From free trade to forced trade : Canada in the global economy / Peter Urmetzer.

Includes index.
ISBN 0-14-100616-1

1. Free trade—Canada. 2. Canada—Economic policy—1991-
3. Canada—Economic conditions—1991- I. Title.

HF1766.U74   2003   382'.71'0971   C2003-900179-2

Visit Penguin Books' website at **www.penguin.ca**

In memory of Anna Doris Urmetzer
1933–2000

Acknowledgements

To START AT THE BEGINNING, I would like to thank John Ralston Saul for introducing me to the staff at Penguin Canada. I would also like to thank the students in my Canadian Society classes at UBC, who relentlessly kept asking questions about free trade, thereby providing the impetus for the writing of this book. Barbara Berson, my initial contact at Penguin, supported the idea from the outset and I am grateful to her for that. Thanks must also go to Desmond Morton and the McGill Institute of Canadian Studies for taking on this project. My editor, the very congenial Susan Folkins, provided many insightful comments about the book's structure. As well, she was positive and optimistic throughout the process, which tended to make me feel likewise. The sharp eye of freelance copy editor Sharon Kirsch kept me on my toes verifying facts, and her comprehensive knowledge of the English language saved me from making many an embarrassing mistake. Sandra Tooze and her staff did an excellent job of proof-reading and editing. Ross Tyner, Sherry MacLeod, and Corky McMechan read sections of the manuscript and provided helpful comments. My father, Martin, and brother, Arno, cooked meals to keep my body nurtured. Also, many thanks to my neighbours, the Burroughs, for cutting my lawn when I was too busy to go outside, and for bringing me soup and cookies. Thanks also to Karen Smallwood and Carl Lakaski for ongoing intellectual and emotional support.

Contents

The most savage controversies are those about matters as
to which there is no good evidence either way.
—BERTRAND RUSSELL

When [all] think alike, no one thinks very much.
—WALTER LIPPMANN

Introduction

UNTIL THE MID-1980s, the topic of international trade received
scant attention from most Canadians. But this would soon
change. Not long after former prime minister Brian Mulroney
was handed his first mandate in 1984, he approached the US
administration about the possibility of entering into a free
trade agreement with Canada. The United States accepted
and talks commenced soon after. Most expected this turn of
events to be the most innocuous of developments, something
left to a handful of trade bureaucrats representing the two
countries involved. After all, the two countries were already
each other's biggest trading partners and trade had increased

1

unabatedly since the Second World War. Surely this trade deal would be nothing more than a formality. To everyone's surprise, however, the process turned out to be anything but, and free trade would become a topic that divided a country. In 1988, for the second time in Canadian history (the first being in 1911), an election effectively served as a plebiscite on a free trade agreement with the United States. Since that time, the topic of international trade has become an increasingly divisive issue not only in Canada but also around the world. As the number of free trade agreements has increased, opposition and acrimony have grown in lockstep. Free trade has inspired people to take to the streets for the first time since the idealistic days of the 1960s and has reinvigorated debates about democratic and civil rights.

Yet for the average Canadian, much confusion exists about the topic and if she does have an opinion, it all too often swings towards the extreme. This ranges from the view that free trade is a panacea for all economic woes to the position that free trade will inevitably lead to corporate rule of the globe: forced trade. Neither view corresponds much with reality, which only makes everyone dig in his heels even deeper. In this battle of persuasion, participants have resorted to everything from hyperbole to fantasy to bolster their cases and steal the limelight. All the while, sober analysis has been left by the wayside.

When it comes to the never-ending struggle to influence public opinion, the pro–free traders seem to be winning. In a survey, conducted on a yearly basis for over a decade now, an increasing number of Canadians agree that free trade has been a good thing for Canada. In 1991, the first time the survey was conducted, shortly after the Canada US Free Trade

Agreement first came into effect, only 47 percent supported free trade, meaning a small majority actually opposed the deal.[1] By 2000, this support had reached a respectable high of 70 percent, likely reflecting satisfaction with a growing economy. In 2001, that support had dropped marginally, to 64 percent, which in all likelihood can be traced to the well-publicized demonstrations that started with the Battle in Seattle and then spread to Windsor, Prague, Genoa, and so on. No doubt, these demonstrations, and even more likely the paramilitary reactions from the organizers of these summits, have compelled some Canadians to reassess their opinion of free trade. On the whole, though, support for free trade has been on the incline over the past decade, and its proponents are likely to evaluate these results with great glee, pointing to a happy marriage between public support and government policy.

The considerable waxing and slight waning of public opinion on this matter raises some interesting questions, the most central being: Why do people choose to support or oppose free trade? More to the point, on what basis do they make such assessments? Survey questions can be notoriously shallow and often raise more questions than they answer. Do respondents support free trade because they themselves or their community has benefited from it? Are respondents generally well informed on the topic, or do they merely come to believe, after more than a decade of endless repetition, what they hear from business leaders and politicians through the media? Can the bulk of support for free trade be traced to centuries-old ideologies? And would further questioning link support to existing political attitudes? Or do people simply fear the alternative to free trade, protectionism? The point is that a survey question that simply asks about free trade fails to answer any of these questions, and we should be careful about relying on public opinion when drawing conclusions about the desirability of free trade. Ideally, we should base these kinds of conclusions on hard scientific data, since the use of public opinion data simply does not make sense. It is like declaring the water in your hometown safe because the majority of citizens believe it to be so.

Yet when we search for hard data about the benefits of free trade, we are likely to walk away unsatisfied. The simple fact is that the evidence shows neither great advantages nor disadvantages. Despite this shaky foundation, both sides have expended considerable energy trying to convince Canadians of the urgency of their cause. Survey results may show that pro–free traders are winning the public relations war, but by no stretch of the imagination does this mean they are any more right. The unexciting reality is that free trade is, economically speaking, a somewhat neutral activity. And this, in a nutshell, is the argument that holds this book together. Short of becoming an autarky and closing its borders completely, a country, no matter how much it trades, is unlikely to become significantly richer or poorer. In other words, the benefits of free trade have been greatly exaggerated by its supporters and its drawbacks have been equally exaggerated by its detractors. As we shall see, there exists no satisfactory evidence that supports either position. Canadian sovereignty has not been compromised because of what many would perceive to be "forced" trade. And despite ubiquitous promises that free trade is going to benefit all those involved, there exists little empirical evidence to back this claim. This is nothing short of remarkable, for it means that one of the primary policy initiatives of the international community, as well as that of individual countries, including Canada, is based more on belief and superstition than an underpinning of solid evidence.

In short, the claim of this book is that all this commotion about trade, in the words of Shakespeare, amounts to "Much ado about nothing," or to use the more contemporary analogy of *Seinfeld*, a political sideshow "about nothing." This is not meant to be insulting to those who protest the ongoing trade meetings or to the bureaucrats who spend endless hours in negotiations, poring over the narcotic details of trade deals. The free trade debate has reached such self-importance that vigilance is required at every step. But this status is greatly undeserved, and the primary objective of this book is to let some air out of this inflated debate.

Second, I hope to critically examine some of the issues that surround free trade with the objective of bringing about a clearer understanding. Not being familiar with the issues often prompts people to jump to conclusions. In the novel *The Caine Mutiny*, Herman Wouk introduces us to a seemingly mad character by the name of Captain Queeg. Queeg's actions are portrayed as those of someone clearly too incompetent to commandeer a warship. Consequently, the reader sympathizes with the crew as it eventually mutinies the captain. But throughout the court case we learn that the case against Queeg is actually quite weak, and as the evidence mounts, readers are forced to reassess their initial judgment. Similarly, I hope to persuade readers that the trade issue is not as black and white as it appears at first blush, and that both sides do have valid concerns.

Last, I seek to assuage some of the fears that people from a wide variety of backgrounds have about free trade. I particularly get this sense from university students, who comprise the majority of demonstrators and are burdened with more than their fair share of pessimism. Much of contemporary politics in Canada is, unfortunately, based on fear, a stick that is used with equal adroitness by both left and right. Canadians are anxious about the deficit, competitiveness, health care, the quality of their food, monopolistic corporations, international trade, and their old age pensions. In what can only be called the politics of fear, people from all walks of life find themselves unnecessarily intimidated into worrying about their future (since most people in Canada have little to worry about in the present). Many of these fears are instigated by politicians, journalists, and commentators of various political stripes. Most Canadians are familiar with refrains like "The World Trade Organization is the new world government" or "If we do not join the global economy our economy will perish."

Not much of a choice, I would say. Yet once people become familiar with the details of these debates, they will find little to fear but the fearmongers themselves, who are ultimately always pushing some kind of agenda. Fortunately or unfortunately, however one chooses to look at it, these fears are mostly without grounds and perpetuated for political reasons: to cut social programs or to protect them, to privatize services or to keep them public. Among these fears, concerns about free trade rate high. It is hoped this book, by clearing up some of the vagueness that surrounds free trade, will allow room for optimism to flourish. This is not meant to be a Pollyannaish "don't worry be happy" kind of analysis, but more of a "I can see clearly now the rain is gone" elucidation.

Protests

The free trade debate is noteworthy because it has revitalized debate along long-established political lines. In recent years, an increasing number of commentators have argued that the old divisions of left and right are no longer meaningful. They point to such developments as workers in the West enjoying an unprecedented standard of living, the collapse of the Soviet Empire, and the fact that political parties of all stripes have followed nearly identical economic policies. On the surface these points appear to be valid. At one time or another, politicians, no matter what their affiliation, whether social democrats like Tony Blair in Great Britain, centrists like Jean Chrétien, or neo-conservatives like Brian Mulroney, have all espoused the benefits of free trade. Yet just because neo-liberalism has infected some important policy issues does not mean everybody is of the same mind, and free trade clearly continues to constitute a division between right and left. The right, as always favouring the efficient mechanism that is the free market, is very much for free anything, including trade. Equally predictable, the left, sometimes purely as an anti-establishment reaction, opposes free trade. Often opposition to free trade originates not in mainstream political parties, but in a seemingly disorganized array of interests, including students, anarchists, unions, and think-tanks. And it is this panoply of interests that has taken the issue of free trade to the streets.

But contemporary protests against free trade are different from the demonstrations of the other great era of protest, the 1960s. Back then, the debates were much simpler to understand. Supporters of the civil rights movement championed the equal treatment of all citizens regardless of ethnic background. People who demonstrated against the war in Vietnam wanted the United States to pull out of Southeast Asia. While there might have been a range of opinions on both these issues, there was never any doubt what exactly they were about. They were simple to understand and it was just as easy to take sides.

In the current debate over free trade, however, the lines of debate are not as easily drawn. One reason is that there are so many issues involved: trade, investment, the environment, intellectual property rights, privatization, sovereignty, culture, Third World debt. Some protesters are demanding what they call managed trade; others, like union members, are afraid their jobs will be jeopardized; still others protest against the high prices that pharmaceutical corporations charge for their wares in the Third World. On top of it all, there is an intimidating list of terms and acronyms that frustrate easy understanding of the issues: countervailing duties, non-tariff barriers, voluntary export restraints, TRIPS, GATS, ITO, MAI, MFN, and the list goes on (for definitions see glossary at the back of the book). This onslaught of jargon has kept many an otherwise-informed citizen from approaching the subject. Consequently, informed discussion has suffered. One of the objects of this book is to clear up some of this confusion.

Canada is one of the most ardent proponents of free trade in the world today, and this is so for good reason. In Canada's five-hundred-year history, trade has been of particular importance. This is typical of smaller economies, which are usually more dependent on trade than their bigger counterparts. The United States, for example, with around 280 million people, has nearly everything it needs to survive comfortably at its disposal: ample natural resources, a vast array of food, sophisticated technologies, and huge markets. In contrast, smaller economies, most notable in terms of geography, depend on trade for many of these products. Some, like Germany and Japan, lack ready access to natural resources such as oil, timber, or iron, and they do well economically only because they are able to trade. Canada, while it has plenty of resources, lacks variety of food, diversity in industry, and large markets that would allow it to function successfully on its own.

For this reason, Canada has always been an enthusiastic supporter of open borders. One could even make the argument that "modern" Canada was created as a trading nation. From the very beginning, its bountiful lands were exploited to satisfy European demand for fish, fur, wheat, and timber. In turn, Canada provided a captive market for European manufactured goods. Over the centuries, the significance of Europe as a trading partner would wane and that of the United States would wax, although the importance of trade itself would remain key. But this dependence, like any dependence, has come at a price. In the past few decades Canada has become increasingly nervous about the United States turning protectionist. Hence, the support for free trade is based less on ideology than sheer necessity. Trade is vital to Canada's economy, which explains, as we shall see throughout the book, why Canada is noticeably more enthusiastic about international trade than most countries.

Some Background Information

There are a few important facts and figures about the global economy in general and the Canadian one in particular that readers need to be familiar with from the outset. Although this book is primarily about Canada and the global economy, it will pay considerable attention to its southern neighbour. This is because the United States is of inordinate importance to Canada's prosperity. Moreover, the United States has been the world's most powerful economy since the Second World War, and continues to be so to this day. This has allowed it to bear undue influence on the world economy. Other countries, such as Germany or Japan, might have come far in the past half century, but neither has been able to challenge American dominance. The United States still comfortably leads the world economy with a gross domestic product (GDP) of over US $8 trillion, easily exceeding that of the next three countries—Japan, Germany, and France—combined. Any story about the world economy, then, must pay special heed to that giant of material wealth, the United States of America.

This is important to Canada for a number of reasons. One, having such a huge economy next door brings with it certain advantages and disadvantages. On the positive side of the ledger, having such a powerful neighbour makes military threats less likely. It also provides Canada with an immense market for its products and offers plenty of opportunities for trade (although this is not automatically a guarantee of riches—look at Mexico). As a matter of fact, the vast majority of Canada's trade, and increasingly so, occurs with our only contiguous neighbour. An impressive 84 percent of Canada's merchandise exports now go to the United States, and 68 percent of imports originate there. In contrast, fewer than 3 percent of our exports go to Japan, and 3 percent of our imports come from Mexico, Canada's next most important trading partners. These figures may seem a bit counterintuitive given all the rhetoric we are exposed to about the globalizing economy, but the simple fact is that since Confederation in 1867, ever more of Canada's trade has been with the United States and increasingly less with the rest of the world. In other words, the Canadian economy is becoming more local (at least in terms of the North American continent) than global. That is not to say this is a bad thing, only to forewarn readers that a book about Canadian trade must necessarily feature the United States as protagonist while everybody else's role is relegated to that of bit player.

Equally important to recognize is the fact that we no longer work and live in an industrial economy but a post-industrial, or service, economy. The majority of Canadians, about three-quarters, now work in the service industry rather than in the production of goods. This has clear consequences for trade, a development the WTO (World Trade Organization) is only too aware of. The bulk of the increase in world trade in the past fifty years has been in goods, whereas the trade in services has stayed remarkably level as a small percentage of the economy. The reason for this is quite simple. Services do not trade well. Services are often consumed close to home, often within walking distance or a short drive. Medical and educational services alone swallow close to one-fifth of Canada's GDP, and most students—the majority of university students and virtually all primary and secondary students—live near to where they consume these services. Likewise, those who are ill visit a clinic or hospital nearby, often purely as a matter of convenience. In addition, even with goods produced outside of the country, the bulk of the price a consumer pays stays within the country. The cost to manufacture a shirt made by the Gap is minimal compared with the expenditure for local

wages (including perfunctory greeting), rents, and advertise-
ments that are incorporated into the final price of the product.
As said, the WTO has realized we have neared the limit of
trade in goods and is now actively planning to increase trade
in services. This quest for free trade in services is responsible
for a number of agreements that come with such inelegant
acronyms as GATS (General Agreement on Trade in Services)
and TRIPS (Agreement on Trade-Related Aspects of
Intellectual Property Rights). How far the WTO is going to be
able to push this agenda is another question. As we shall see
throughout the book, the external world often tends to behave
independently of our wishes, and when it comes to trade in
services, wishful thinking is likely to remain just that.

Readers should also be aware of the general shape of the
post-war economy. For the first few decades following the
Second World War, the global economy, which really means
that of the First World, grew at its fastest pace ever. This
period is often referred to as the Golden Age of Capitalism.
But as with all good things, this also had to end. In this
instance, the sheen started to dull in about the mid-1970s.
Since then, economic growth has lagged. Some people may
find this counterintuitive, particularly with the respectable
growth the United States was able to post during the 1990s.
The fact is, though, the United States does not a world
economy make, and by any means, that growth was not as
rapid as it was during the 1950s and 1960s. More important,
wages in both Canada and the United States have stagnated
since the gold turned to lead. Median family income in
Canada has virtually remained flat since the mid-1970s,
whereas it more than doubled throughout the 1950s and
1960s. In that sense, the halcyon days are gone, and as most

Canadians are able to attest, economically speaking, things could be better.

Obsession: Not Just a Perfume

One of the arguments in this book is that the ongoing quest for free trade, given its paltry benefits, borders on the irrational. Here an analogy should prove instructive. We are all familiar with the fact that people can become obsessive in their behaviour. This ranges from the innocuous, like paying your bills on time, to more harmful behaviour that can include compulsive handwashing, chronic worrying about one's health, or unjustified concerns over one's physical appearance. But obsession is not the exclusive domain of individuals and can just as easily afflict institutions, as the following example illustrates.

In the mid-1970s Canada first began to implement a high-interest, low-inflation policy that culminated in nothing less than an obsession in the early 1990s. Some further explanation is in order. In Canada, as in most industrial economies, the organization responsible for controlling inflation is the central bank. In the United States this duty is performed by the Federal Reserve, in Germany the Bundesbank, and in Canada the Bank of Canada. The major policy tool a central bank has at its disposal to manage inflation is higher interest rates. When inflation increases, higher interest rates are usually enough to contain it. For whatever it is worth, high interest rates were effective in bringing down inflation from a high of 12.4 percent in 1981 to below 5 percent throughout the majority of the mid- and late 1980s. The reasoning behind the fight against inflation is that stable prices make for a stable economy. But the case against inflation is often based on extremes. Most people are familiar with the pain associated with hyperinflation as was experienced in Germany between the two world wars. But a rate of 5 percent hardly qualifies as excessive. Even conservative institutions like the World Bank have admitted that single-digit inflation, anything below 10 percent, has in no demonstrable way an adverse effect on the economy. However, and for whatever reason, John Crowe, governor of the Bank of Canada from 1987 to 1994, decided if hyperinflation was bad, then inflation of any sort was bad, and embarked Canada on a zero-percent inflation policy. He pursued this goal with obsessive zealousness. Like a germ-phobic Howard Hughes, John Crowe's logic was that if a lot of something was bad, then a little must be bad, too. There would be no room for moderation, and zero inflation became an end in itself, without regard for the damage that high interest rates might inflict on the economy. Carried along by his obsession, Crowe was successful in wrestling the inflation rate to below 2 percent in the early 1990s. At one point, in 1993, it went as low as 0.2 percent. But at what cost?

On the positive side Canada had stable prices, which, like plenty of trade, might not give all that much of a thrill to most people. The negative side of this policy was more apparent. As interest rates rose, the cost of borrowing deterred business and consumers from investing, which in turn meant fewer people were employed. This can easily be demonstrated on an individual level. When interest rates are high, a family is less likely to purchase a home because mortgage payments will also be high. This has an immediate and negative effect on the economy, as fewer construction workers are employed: electricians, framers, plumbers; even lawyers, surveyors, and city planners. When a family decides against building a house, all this labour sits idle. And so it went for the first half of the 1990s. For the six years spanning 1990 to 1995 the number of building permits, both commercial and residential, dropped for each year but one. The same was true for investment in general, as high interest rates meant that all debts, including government debt, grew rapidly. There is overwhelming evidence that shows the so-called debt and deficit crisis that caused so many government programs to be cut was very much exacerbated by high interest rates.[2] High interest rates also negatively affected the Third World, a topic we will revisit in detail below. And all of this for the intangible benefit of extirpating inflation.

This, then, is a perfect example of an institution becoming obsessive and losing sight of the larger picture. There are, unfortunately, too many examples of this. The obsession with law and order, as has been the case in the United States in recent years, has resulted in hundreds of thousands of people being sent to jail for doing drugs, something that should be considered a health problem rather than a criminal one. Police departments often develop a compulsion to find a perpetrator and many an innocent person has been convicted. Donald Marshall, David Milgaard, and Steven Truscott are only a few examples of this in Canada's recent history.

Everywhere we look, we are faced with institutions that have become obsessive and have lost sight of the consequences of their actions. Whether it is the eradication of inflation or the need to enforce the law, politicians and bureaucrats forget why they implement policies and focus on the means. The pursuit of free trade in the past two decades, not only in Canada but also around the world, serves as just another example of this type of institutional madness.

The Big Idea

Free trade is nothing more than the Big Idea of the late twentieth century. A Big Idea is not necessarily planned, and as
appears to be the case in this instance, is just as likely to be
stumbled upon. Many Big Ideas have humble beginnings and
may not work all that well at first, but eventually they catch
on and create a momentum of their own. It does not hurt that
the Big Idea of free trade has a respectable pedigree, validated
by the writings of such venerable thinkers as Adam Smith and
David Ricardo. Over the centuries this idea has become so
much part of the folklore of capitalism that it seems beyond
reproach. Repetition of the message eventually wears people
down and shuts down their critical faculties. After all, if well-
informed politicians and policy-makers believe it, the public
reasons, it must be true.

The Big Idea of free trade, like many Big Ideas, appeals
to politicians in that it seemingly provides a simple solution to
many of our social and economic ailments. Slowing economic
growth: free trade. Third World poverty: free trade. Lagging
productivity: free trade. High unemployment: free trade.
Political unrest in poor countries: free trade. The beauty of
free trade is that ultimately politicians are seen as doing
something when in fact they are doing nothing. "Free" as in
free market, after all, means that governments need not do
anything. Any problem that arises can be solved simply by
leaving it alone, or in this case, having more free trade. If a
policy fails to work, it can be blamed on the cruel but necessary discipline of the market; if it succeeds, it provides all the
more reason to have more free markets. To do nothing, which
is actually a choice, becomes *the* policy option.

Road Map: Organization of the Book

First, we are going to take a detailed look at the theory of free trade and question some of the assumptions that underlie it. Chapter 1 looks at some evidence in order to assess whether or not free trade has actually brought about the benefits promised by its supporters. The world is a much different place than it was in the eighteenth and nineteenth centuries when the theory of free trade was first conceived, and this raises questions about its applicability at the beginning of the third millennium. The next four chapters cover the history of free markets in general and Canada's economic history in particular. Both are necessary for a thorough understanding of how free trade plays out in contemporary Canadian society. The two are also inextricably linked. The idea of free trade originated in Great Britain over two centuries ago and from there was exported to the colonies, including Canada, and then to the rest of the world. Throughout the book, and specifically in chapters 2, 3, and 4, the reader will be introduced to three economists with whom most readers will at least have a passing familiarity. Chronologically, they are Adam Smith, David Ricardo, and John Maynard Keynes. All three were British and all three continue, for better or worse, to have a profound impact on the way the world economy is structured today. This does not, however, mean that they were any more right or that any of their ways were better. As a matter of fact, I am going to stress that the ideas generally associated with these economists are not generalizable to all times and places because they are historically and geographically specific. Too often, these writings, particularly of the classical economists (Smith, Ricardo), are taken out of the historical context in which these authors lived. Furthermore, selective quotes ignore the subtlety of their thinking. By providing a historical backdrop, I hope that readers will arrive at a better understanding of what motivated Smith and Ricardo to advocate free markets. We will also meet Keynes, who, in turn, challenged the free market doctrines of the classical economists in a way that was palatable to most Western governments.

Modern Canada was established as a trading nation and its natural resources were exploited by it colonizers from the very beginning, first by France and then by England. The importance of trade to the Canadian economy has not faded since. Chapter 5 will show how important foreign markets have been and continue to be to the Canadian economy. Still, Canada has gone through long periods of relative protectionism with no discernible negative impact on its economy. Chapter 6 is primarily about the WTO. The chapter traces the trials and tribulations of the institution and how it got to be where it is today. The chapter also presents the nuts and bolts of various trade agreements: tariffs, duties, subsidies, subagreements. Chapter 7 presents a series of case studies in order to illustrate the difficulties that the WTO and enforcers of other free trade agreements face. This is most apparent when it comes to the environment, as there exists an interminable tension between production and the environment, and consequently between environmentalists and free traders. The crux of the problem is that environmental laws often turn out to be a disguised form of protectionism, and it is difficult to ascertain when a trade ban is based on legitimate environmental concerns and when it serves as a convenient excuse to protect domestic industry. The chapter will also touch on such contentious issues as state sovereignty and the feasibility of having an international organization making decisions about health and safety standards.

Free trade is an issue that is integral to the relationship between the First and Third worlds. Chapter 8 examines how the IMF (International Monetary Fund), the World Bank, and the WTO have attempted to create a world after their own images. This chapter is quite critical of free trade and highlights how the two industries in which the Third World is most competitive, agriculture and textiles, have been wilfully ignored by the WTO. In chapter 9 we revisit some theoretical issues and highlight one of the most overlooked aspects of free trade: production and employment. And finally, the conclusion makes some speculation as to the future of free trade in Canada.

In sum, it will be shown that free trade is more of an ideology than a policy built on a foundation of solid evidence. The best place to begin our study is to take a detailed look at the theory of free trade itself. What are its supposed benefits? Its pitfalls? And how do expectations about its success, or failure, square with the evidence? It is these details that we shall turn our attention to next.

1

Economics is a subject that does not
greatly respect one's wishes.
—NIKITA KHRUSHCHEV

FREE TRADE:
THEORY AND PRACTICE

WHY TRADE? At one level, there are many obvious benefits to
be gleaned from this activity. In Canada, a sometimes harsh
climate means that food production is interrupted for a significant portion of the year. Only because of imports are we able
to enjoy fresh fruits and vegetables all year. Canadians also
benefit from trade in other ways and are able to purchase a
multitude of products from around the world: sleek European
sports cars, clothes and textiles from Asia, carpets from Iran
and Afghanistan, coffee from South America, and the list goes
on. But on another level, there is good reason to question the
benefits of free trade. Most of Canada's trade is with other
industrial countries (the United States, Japan) and in products
we could easily manufacture ourselves. Furthermore, we have

had free trade in Canada for well over a dozen years now, and many of the promises that were made have not come to fruition. Yet the Canadian government is continuing to pursue this policy with considerable vigour. It is time to take stock.

Trust Me, It's Good for You

When Prime Minister Tony Blair of Britain addressed the Canadian Parliament in February 2001, he spoke of the urgency of opening up borders. To quote: "[Free trade is] the key to jobs for our people, prosperity and actually to development in the poorest parts of the world."[3] In an editorial about Blair's speech, *The Globe and Mail* was compelled to add that "Poor countries that join the global economy through trade invariably become richer over time."[4] Such insights have become a steady diet for news readers around the world, promulgated by institutions like the WTO, private enterprise, journalists, and interest groups disguised as think-tanks. Given this consensus on the benefits of free trade, we would expect to find irrefutable documentation of its superiority. Yet there is scant evidence to corroborate that open borders are beneficial to either individual economies or the world economy as a whole. If there were such evidence, proponents of free trade would most surely cite it, and endlessly so. But there is a noticeable silence on this issue, for such a study does not exist. The introduction presented some evidence from public opinion surveys that showed support for free trade has increased over the past decade. But we also concluded that this sort of evidence cannot be considered an accurate barometer of the desirability of free trade. For that, we will have to examine more scientific details such as economic growth, job losses and gains, and seemingly unrelated variables like high interest rates and an aging population. Only such a background will allow us to accurately assess the claims made about free trade by both proponents and opponents alike.

Every time a politician the likes of Blair or Mulroney extols the benefits of free trade, one wonders what evidence these observations are based on. Usually such statements are more a matter of faith, and evidence is relegated to only a minor role if not ignored altogether. This is somewhat surprising, given all the hyperbole we hear about the benefits of free trade. Since countries have put so much energy into opening their borders, we should expect at least some documentation that substantiates the benefits of free trade. But such evidence is signally missing, making one wonder why.

One would think that the results of free trade are easy to measure, but such an endeavour is, as we shall see, much more complicated than first appears. In order to ensure that we conduct our investigation properly, we are going to take a cue from Albert Einstein. Einstein explicated that modern science is based on two basic principles: one, the theorizing of a general relationship of dependence between two events; and, two, the subsequent testing of these theories through experimentation. This line of reasoning is a hallmark of modern science, and it is also the logic that will guide this chapter. Unfortunately, we are unable to test the free trade theory through experiment, given the difficulty of getting consent and all that. Still, we are well advised to keep in mind Einstein's first principle, which underscores the importance of positing a relationship between two events. For our investigation, this relationship can be summarized as follows: Free trade causes, leads to, or correlates highly with—whichever language one chooses to use—positive economic growth. Throughout this chapter we are going to think about the evidence in light of this relationship, which should point us either to or away from the plausibility of such a relationship.

Before we assess the evidence, let us briefly look at a typical example of how the benefits of free trade are usually presented. Gordon Ritchie, one of the chief negotiators for the Canada US Free Trade Agreement, admits to not having done all that well when studying economics. Despite this, or maybe because of it, he is an unrepentant defender of free trade. He writes that "the theory [of free trade] was as robust as economic analysis could ever be."[5] Furthermore, he acknowledges that the superiority of free trade "was a given" when he worked for the minister of trade and commerce. As evidence of the benefits of free trade, he casually alludes to the rapid post-war growth. In contrast, in order to demonstrate the folly of closed borders, he directs our attention to the rising protectionism that ensued during the Depression. Many free traders, including Ritchie, contend that the Smoot Hawley Tariff, introduced by the Americans in 1930, either caused or at least greatly aggravated the severity of the Depression. Both these points—that free trade leads to rapid economic expansion and protectionism invariably leads down the road to economic ruin—are commonly used as a defence for free trade, and it behooves us to examine these claims in some detail.

Post-War Growth

First and foremost, the reader should realize that the benefits of free trade are purely theoretical. Free trade is just a theory about how the economic world works and the effect that one variable bears on another. In the most simple terms, and keeping in mind Einstein's observations, free traders assume that an increase in one variable (free trade) results in an increase in another (income, economic growth, or wealth). Not surprisingly, anti–free traders take pretty much the opposite position and propose that free trade leads to higher unemployment, lower wages, and, hence, slower economic growth, although they add the important proviso that benefits accrue to the already wealthy. In any case, both sides work within the trade/growth framework, the difference being that those who support free trade argue that a positive relationship exists between the two variables and those who oppose it imagine this relationship to be negative. Theoretically neither of these propositions is difficult to understand; neither represents a complicated relationship. Maybe that explains their appeal. But just because a model is theoretically simple does not mean the world automatically falls into place to accommodate it.

Supporters of free trade know few bounds when it comes to their enthusiasm for open markets. In order to bolster their case they attribute all kinds of wonderful things to free trade. The WTO traces the post-war peace to the claim that trading nations do not fight, although there is scant evidence to support this. European countries traded vigorously from 1910 to 1913, yet they fought the First World War anyway. Free traders also like to credit the post-war boom to the parallel increase in trade. Yet tariffs were still relatively high in the beginning of that era, and now that they have been substantially lowered, economic growth has also slowed. Again, such evidence taxes the credibility of the free trade theory. Furthermore, there are many instances, including Canada's National Policy of 1879, where protectionist policies were practised for over a century without apparent ill effects to the economy. Even this cursory overview illustrates that the theory of free trade takes some questionable liberties when it comes to tracing its benefits.

The fact that the evidence for the benefits of free trade is, at best, tenuous has failed to dissuade both opponents and proponents from their respective causes. The belief of the superiority of free trade is deeply ingrained into the psyches of its supporters. But since substantiating data are hard to come by, proponents have been compelled to circumvent the cause and effect relationship altogether. Instead, researchers have resorted to fuzzy logic and selective evidence to back their claims. Rather than measuring the success of free trade by economic growth, which, arguably, should be its ultimate objective, researchers marshal statistics showing the amount of goods and services traded. As evidence of the success of a series of bilateral trade negotiations between the United States and selected countries after the Second World War, Michael Hart, a senior associate of the Centre for Trade Policy and Law at Carleton University provides *trade* statistics and writes that "Economically, the program was a success."[6] In other words, increased trade is presented as evidence of the success of a free trade agreement, which is questionable to begin with, but to further characterize this as an economic success is disingenuous, as it conflates increased trade with economic well-being. Similarly, Sidney Weintraub contends that the proper way to assess the success of a free trade agreement, in this case the North American Free Trade Agreement (NAFTA), is to measure the amount of trade that has transpired under the new trade regime.[7] This makes one wonder why have free trade if its sole benefit is more trade? These are not isolated examples but are indi ..ive of an emerging trend, noted by Graham Dunkley, in which trade is no longer a means to an end (economic growth), but an end in itself.[8] In this sleight of hand, free trade and economic growth become synonymous. Free trade is economic success. No need to examine further evidence about economic growth, as trade itself becomes the objective. This melding of the free trade/growth relationship conveniently circumvents any difficulties that one might have showing the relationship between the variables of free trade and economic growth. Voluminous trade is economic success. Full stop.

Not surprisingly, the relationship between trade and economic growth has proven much more difficult to verify empirically. For this, let us examine what turned out to be a heated topic of discussion throughout the free trade debate in Canada in the late 1980s: jobs. One of the rallying cries during the campaign for free trade, a period of high unemployment, was the promise of more and better employment. Jobs in this case can easily stand as a proxy for our dependent variable, economic growth. In Canada, proponents of free trade point to an increase in trade with the United States in order to demonstrate its benefits, and from there make all kinds of extrapolations about the jobs that have been created. Brian Mulroney writes that "trade means jobs [and it] has created four of every five new jobs since 1993."[9] Of course, this argument completely ignores the jobs destroyed by free trade. Enumerating jobs created while ignoring those lost is akin to giving only half the score in a hockey game. And no one can deny that there are two sides to this story, that free trade cost at least some jobs. As American branch plants relocated to their home base, jobs went with them. At the heart of the issue is whether the jobs lost were replaced or exceeded by the jobs created. Put slightly differently, has there been a net gain or net loss in jobs? This is a critical point, and while it may be difficult to confirm, it does not make for very good science to ignore it. In other words, in the absence of free trade, Canada would in all likelihood be manufacturing more products for the domestic market, which would mean fewer exports but at the same time fewer imports. The resulting wealth could well be comparable, if not identical. A similar criticism can be made of studies that point to the number of jobs that have disappeared because of free trade. They ignore the number of jobs that have been created in export industries. A job loss in the tire industry might have been replaced with a job in car manufacturing, a job in the fruit industry with one in the wine industry. In the end it becomes impossible to keep track of how many jobs have been created and how many have been destroyed and to arrive at an accurate net figure.

Furthermore, not all jobs are the same and how does one compare jobs lost with those gained? Is a job gained in the service industry selling books equivalent to a job lost assembling tractors? How does one assess good jobs and bad jobs and should such a distinction be drawn in the first place? The issue gets even more complicated. Even if one were able to arrive at some reasonable estimate of net job losses or gains, it would be a logical leap to then attribute this change to free trade. Let us refocus our attention on our original relationship between free trade and economic growth. There are so many other factors that dilute the impact of free trade that it not only overwhelms our minds but also confounds statistical models. The post-war economy will serve as an instructive example. In both Canada and the West, the economy experienced rapid growth in the immediate post-war era up until about 1975. As a matter of fact, this period was the most prosperous ever for the world economy, Canada included, and consequently is frequently referred to as the Golden Age. After 1975, that growth slowed, again not only in Canada but around the world. But to blame that slower growth on free trade would be unfair. Many other factors contributed: Mechanization made many jobs redundant and employment opportunities decreased dramatically in primary industries, such as forestry and mining, and secondary industries, such as manufacturing.

In other words, throughout the decades following the Second World War, the rich economies underwent a transition from industrial to post-industrial, or service, economies. On top of some misguided political decisions, this has meant a sea change in the composition of the labour market, from well-paying and secure manufacturing jobs to part-time and temporary service jobs. Canadians are also much better educated now. Those with little education are faring worse than their uneducated predecessors of the 1950s, and the chasm between the less educated and the well educated is continually widening. In short, Canada's labour market is becoming increasingly polarized, and while it is able to boast some very good service jobs (lawyers, engineers, teachers), there are just as many, if not more, less desirable ones (clerks, short-order cooks, telemarketers). Meanwhile, the number of well-paying industrial job markets is decreasing steadily. Technology appears to have played a more important role in this realignment of jobs than has free trade.

If this were not already complex enough, other factors need to be considered. Millions of baby boomers are at a point in their lives when they are no longer buying big-ticket items and investing their savings in the stock and money markets. Booming stock markets in the 1980s and 1990s are a testament to this. As millions of people have voluntarily curtailed their consumption over the past decades, fewer people are needed to produce goods. And so the list that explains the economic downturn goes on seemingly without end: The energy crisis in the 1970s meant that inflation firmly entrenched itself into the economy; high interest rates to fight inflation led to increased unemployment; increased private debt meant consumers had less discretionary money to spend, which further contributed to unemployment; mounting debt has forced all levels of government to lay off workers and implement cutbacks; a lower dollar has led to higher costs for imports; shrinking incomes has meant that one-income families are no longer viable, compelling an unprecedented number of women to join the workforce in order to make up for the shortfall.

Now comes the difficult task of determining whether the economic slump of the past decades was due to free trade, a general downturn in the business cycle, jobs devoured by technology, a trend towards a post-industrial economy, a slow-down in consumption by baby boomers, or demographic changes such as an aging population or smaller families. In other words, we need to establish a relationship between free trade and the economic decline. The above only hints at the huge inventory of variables that can be implicated here. Furthermore, variables often interact and it is difficult some-times to tell which is cause and which is effect. Is unemploy-ment the result of a slowing economy or is the slowing economy a manifestation of increased unemployment?

Shrinking wages have meant that those with jobs are working longer hours, which has directly translated into a falling demand for workers, higher unemployment, and even lower wages. This reveals that variables interact, and as seems to be the case here, once everything impacts everything else we are stuck in an epistemological nowhere land. This is further complicated by the fact that there has been relatively little change in the dependent variable, economic growth (measured according to gross domestic product, or GDP). Since the mid-1970s, the Canadian economy has neither crashed nor regained its Golden Age splendour. In other words, how can trade be responsible for an increase in economic growth when there has been no substantial increase in that economic growth? As a matter of fact, growth has slowed, but, admittedly, not drastically enough to be able to link to a specific variable. Unfortunately for both those who support and oppose free trade, when it comes to the relationship between trade and economic growth, the evidence is far too thin to draw any definitive conclusions. And given the relatively small changes in economic growth that we have experienced in the post-war economy, it is more likely that it is the effect of trade that has been negligible rather than our inability to detect that change.

The variables just examined point to two important conclusions. One, the rapid post-war growth cannot be directly linked to free trade. As a public policy issue, with the exception of the General Agreement on Tariffs and Trade (GATT) negotiations, free trade was very much on the back burner throughout the first three decades after the Second World War. This resulted in relatively little trade, yet economic growth was substantially more robust than now. Variables like high employment, vast increases in productivity, and a better educated workforce were obviously much more consequential here than free trade. Two, the gradual contraction of the economy that began in the mid-1970s cannot be blamed on free trade either. Again, there are many other variables that can be implicated and probably had a more profound impact. If the effects of free trade are likely to be negligible, why has there been all this commotion for nearly twenty years? This is difficult to say, but it is likely that the free trade enthusiasm itself was brought about by a slowing economy. As markets around the world, including Canada's, became saturated, unimaginative politicians and bureaucrats found it easiest to offer some platitudes about free markets. Such a policy is always easy to follow and involves essentially nothing more than putting one's faith in some supernatural force. In this case, little action has resulted in little change, just what the safe politician ordered.

The Statistical Relationship between Trade and Growth

That the relationship between trade and growth is dubious can also be demonstrated via statistics. Relationships such as this are usually measured using tests bearing esoteric Greek names, but if the relationship is strong there is often no need to rely on sophisticated statistical procedures. For example, there exists a strong relationship between education and income. When parents urge their children to attend university, it is not because they want someone to discuss literature with but because they believe it is one of the best ways to guarantee a well-paying job. Most people know this intuitively and there is no need to convince them by trotting out reams of numbers. While this relationship is not a perfect one—that is, it does not universally hold true, as a logger with no education might earn more than a PhD working for a non-profit organization—it is, nevertheless, a strong one. On the other hand, an example of a weak or non-existent relationship would be that between hair colour and IQ. Surprisingly, an equally weak relationship is found between trade and growth. When we examine these data for Canada for the past fifty years—specifically, the amount of trade in a year as a percentage of GDP and the percentage growth of the GDP for that same year—we find there is no positive relationship at all. As a matter of fact, the relationship is slightly negative (although not statistically significant). As is often the case with statistical relationships, including the one between education and income just discussed, this one, too, can easily be demonstrated without the use of elaborate formulas. During the Golden Age, from 1945 to 1975, Canada traded relatively little and its economy grew rapidly, as said, the fastest ever. From 1975 until the present, no doubt as a result of the string of trade agreements introduced, trade grew at a much faster rate, yet at the same time economic growth slowed. So the position that free trade increases wealth is difficult to sustain. Certainly, as discussed, there are many other factors that contributed to the downturn in the economy, but these observations clearly put into doubt the trade/growth relationship. There is scant evidence that free trade, as Mr. Blair professes, provides jobs and generates economic growth.

Smoot Hawley Tariff

Nietzsche observed that we criticize others in order to make ourselves look better. Free traders have taken this advice to heart and are quick to disparage all alternatives to their cause. To show that free trade is good, its proponents have felt compelled to vilify its opposite—protectionism, or the closing of borders to imports—to no end. It has come to pass that the most frequently cited example of protectionism is the Great Depression. This event, which began in the late 1920s and lasted well into the mid-1930s, is often used as a fear tactic to convince people that free trade is the only option.

Many commentators have put forward the opinion, often taken to be historical fact, that the worldwide Depression of the 1930s was, if not caused by the surge in protectionism, at least significantly exacerbated by it. Free traders like Gordon Ritchie trot out this example uncritically and without evidence. And as we just saw with the theory of free trade, the evidence here is not all that convincing either. When considering the relationship between two variables, it is essential to keep in mind the importance of time ordering. If protectionism did indeed cause the Depression, then the former must obviously have preceded the latter in time. Given this observation, we can be certain that the Smoot Hawley Tariff—the legislation that imposed high tariffs on all imports—did not cause the Depression, as by the time it became law, on June 17, 1930, the economic downturn was already well underway. Even the stock market crash in October 1929, the event most commonly associated with ushering in the Depression, was only a manifestation of the slump, not its cause. By the summer of 1929, retail sales, manufacturing, and construction were already down sharply in the United States, as were commodity prices in Canada, including those of wheat and newsprint. Most important, credit was tight, a hangover from the costs associated with the First World War. Germany was unable to make good on its reparation payments, Britain itself was no longer capable of being the lender to the world, and there was no other country willing or able to take its place. Finally, the further tightening of credit, required to cool down an overheated stock market, overburdened the already rickety world financial system and caused it to collapse.[10]

The downturn in trade might have played a more central role in a trade-dependent country like Canada, but it was less important a factor in the United States itself, the country responsible for introducing the Smoot Hawley Tariff. In 1929, American exports amounted to only 7 percent of GNP and imports to 6.3 percent. This means that foreign trade played only a minor role in the huge US economy. Trade did collapse by approximately two-thirds (to 2.4 percent of GNP for exports and 2.3 for imports), but it would border on the fantastic to trace a 50 percent drop in GNP to an activity relatively peripheral to the economy. Put slightly differently, of all industrial economies the country that traded the least, the United States, was also hit hardest by the Depression. Even if the Smoot Hawley Tariff had not been implemented, the Americans would have traded fewer goods because their economy was in free fall. As mentioned, the financial system was in ruins around the world and particularly in the United States, where almost 10 000 banks failed. This had a far more profound impact on the economy than a decrease in trade. A lack of demand for products inside the United States and elsewhere meant the economy slowed, tariff or no tariff.

Some economists are rightfully skeptical of the relationship between the erection of tariffs and economic growth in general, and the Smoot Hawley Tariff and the Depression in particular. Paul Krugman has gone as far as calling this theoretical relationship "nonsense."[11] All the same, this myth persists, a fantasy that Dunkley refers to as the "Legend of the Thirties."[12] Yet the tariffs implemented in the 1930s are often presented as a stick to demonstrate the dangers of protectionism. But such claims are largely unfounded, for a moderate amount of protectionism is unlikely to result in economic ruin. Krugman estimates that if world trade were reduced by 50 percent, world output (GDP for all countries combined) would decrease only by 2.5 percent.[13] Again, not something to lose sleep over.

Historical Evidence

Another way to examine the effects of trade is to follow the historical route. There should be no shortage of data, as the world is a big place and capitalism has been around for almost half a millennium. Given the confidence with which free traders argue, we would expect to be able to cherry-pick examples from the past where countries that chose free trade over protectionism prospered, letting those ignorant of its obvious benefits wallow in their self-imposed squalor. But again, this kind of evidence is wanting.

We are going to examine Canada's history in more detail in chapter 5, but for our present purposes a quick overview of Canada's and Europe's past trade practices will suffice. The fact is that modern Canada itself was a product of planned markets, and actually involved very little "free" trade. Goods, such as fish and lumber, were essentially taken from North America without permission. Europeans did engage in trade, but only when no other option presented itself. This is true of the fur trade, in which case Europeans depended on the co-operation of Aboriginals, without which they surely would have perished. Furthermore, trade in all products, not only furs, was monopolized, as France (and later Britain) was determined that no other country or corporation should have access to these markets. As the economy evolved into an agricultural and industrial one, the assistance of Aboriginals was no longer needed and they were displaced as their land was used for farming and resource extraction. These processes all occurred without permission, and if the Aboriginals were compensated, the sums were always paltry. The majority of these goods—timber, wheat, minerals—then found their way back to the colonizing countries. In turn, the European countries sold manufactured goods back to Canada. But this arrangement, although it benefited the European countries tremendously, could hardly be called free trade. It was more akin to forced trade, as many of these products were taken under, to be overly generous, coercive conditions. In that sense, the British Empire engaged more in racketeering than free trade.

Now, let us take a closer look at the British Empire, often heralded as a model for the benefits of free trade. Free trade was indeed first introduced to Great Britain, but not until 1846. By that time, the British Empire was already near its apex of economic dominance, a result not of free trade but of exploitation of its colonies, both for natural resources and markets. Before 1846, the British state was more interventionist than any contemporary government and probably rivalled that of the centrally planned economies of the erstwhile Soviet Union. Success was firmly built on monopoly. The only large-scale businesses of the day, the equivalents of contemporary corporations, were run by governments. These organizations were anything but competitive, as they were granted exclusive trading rights in the colonies. The Hudson's Bay Company and the English East India Company are well-known examples of this. Under the Navigation Acts, even transportation of goods to and from the colonies was monopolized. Protected markets and nepotism meant markets were anything but free.

Thus Great Britain arrived at the height of its economic and industrial dominance via tightly controlled markets. But that dominance would soon be challenged as other countries were also industrializing. Between 1870 and 1913, the growth of Great Britain's economy started to lag behind that of the United States. This was particularly the case in the production of steel, chemicals, and later automobiles. During that period, the growth rate for the United States was a respectable 5 percent per annum, more than double that of Great Britain, which experienced a much less impressive 2 percent per annum.[14] One should not put too fine a point on this, for as we saw above, there are many other factors that can be implicated when it comes to explaining fluctuations in economic growth. On the other hand, though, it is worthwhile noting that throughout these years the United States was in the midst of a long period of protectionism. While it may be unfair to blame the slower growth of the British economy on free trade, this new policy obviously did not perform any wonders for Britain's economy either.

Neither can the respectable growth of the United States any time before the Second World War—when it snatched away from Great Britain the title of the most powerful economy in the world—be linked to free trade. The fact is that the United States became increasingly protectionist from when it first became independent in 1776 right up until the mid-1930s when it began to slowly dismantle the Smoot Hawley Tariff. Similarly, Canada enjoyed a century of unprecedented prosperity under the protectionist National Policy without any apparent ill effects on its economy. Although this evidence is far from conclusive, it casts serious doubt on the claim that countries that practise free trade have historically outperformed those that protected their markets.

Despite this perspicuous lack of evidence, supporters of free trade continue to champion their cause around the world. Not only do existing free trade agreements continue to be in place, but ongoing negotiations are destined to lead to further and more comprehensive trade deals. This raises the question why. In order to find an answer to this question, we cannot appeal to logic or evidence but must turn to history. In the next two chapters we are going to follow the roots of free trade and highlight the work of two of its most famous proponents, Adam Smith and David Ricardo, usually referred to as the classical economists. By taking a close look at their writings, we are better able to comprehend their enthusiasm for free markets as well as to evaluate how applicable these ideas are in the contemporary world.

2

It is not from the benevolence of the butcher, the brewer, or the baker that we expect our dinner, but from their regard to their self-interest. We address ourselves, not to their humanity, but to their self-love, and never talk to them of our necessities, but of their advantages.
—ADAM SMITH

No society can surely be flourishing and happy, of which the far greater part of the members are poor and miserable.
—ADAM SMITH

ADAM SMITH:
THE FREE MARKET REVEALED

THE PURPORTED ADVANTAGES that are associated with free markets are deeply embedded in the psyches of our collective consciousness. As we just saw, free trade continues to be actively promoted throughout the world despite a questionable track record. This is particularly true in English-speaking countries, Canada included. Although there has been a resurgence of free trade in the past couple of decades, arguments about its benefits are far from new and can boast a long and impressive pedigree. Unfortunately, understanding of these ideas is often superficial. In order to critically appraise them, we need to know more about the historical circumstances in which they originated.

Considered one of the major figures of the Scottish Enlightenment, Adam Smith wrote in the second half of the eighteenth century and is best known for his economic treatise *The Wealth of Nations* (1776). Smith's writings are far-reaching, yet his reputation primarily rests on his rejection of state intervention. He supported free markets at a time when few did, and consequently he has become a favourite of conservative commentators who invoke him at every opportunity. The author of one of the most cogent defences of the free market ever offered, Smith is better known more than two centuries after his death than are most of his contemporary brethren. The fact that he coined the very powerful metaphor of the "invisible hand" to symbolize free markets only further contributes to his fame. Smith is referred to so often, including in the mainstream media, that even people with no formal knowledge of economics or philosophy are likely to have heard of him.

It is regrettable that Smith's name has come to be so closely associated with conservative economics and anti-state sentiments, for he was generally a very broad thinker. Along the lines of Karl Marx and John Stuart Mill, whose writings comfortably stretched across several disciplines, Smith was a capacious thinker. All these philosophers' writings touched upon ethics, economics, sociology, political science, and in the case of Smith, even astronomy. Thus the probability is high that the typical undergraduate student will come across

Smith's writings somewhere in the course of his education, even if only superficially. And again like Marx's, Smith's thinking is markedly more subtle and sophisticated than either critics or supporters give him credit for. It is particularly said of Smith that he is often quoted and seldom read. This is revealed by the fact that Smith is frequently relied upon to defend open markets, although he was just as concerned about the welfare of the common labourer.

Smith was born in 1723 in Kircaldy, Scotland, and educated at the universities of Glasgow and Oxford. It is worth pointing out that Smith was not an economist as such, nor did he ever formally teach a course in economics. Smith was trained as a philosopher, and any economics he did teach was incorporated into his lectures on philosophy.[15] Smith had the good fortune of becoming famous within his lifetime, and first gained national attention with his *Theory of Moral Sentiments* (1759). His following work, *An Inquiry into the Nature and Causes of the Wealth of Nations*, took well over a decade to write and was published in 1776, the same year the American colonies signed the Declaration of Independence.

As the title of his book indicates, Smith was primarily concerned about how wealth was measured. In this he differed from the prevailing opinion of the day. Rather than being a conservative apologist for the merchant class, he chided their ignorance. *The Wealth* was first and foremost an attack against mercantilism, a theory of international trade practised by Great Britain at the time. The theory was founded on the belief that wealth could be measured by the accumulation of gold and silver. But Smith argued that it was not the amount of bullion stored away in vaults that reflected a country's wealth, but rather the general standard of living enjoyed by its citizens.

In *The Wealth* Smith continued to expound on self-interest, a topic that he first wrote about in *Moral Sentiments*, where he put forward the idea that if everybody did what she thought was in her best interest, the common good would prevail. "It is not from the benevolence of the butcher, the brewer, or the baker that we expect our dinner, but from their regard to their self-interest. We address ourselves, not to their humanity, but to their self-love, and never talk to them of our necessities, but of their advantages."[16] Central to Smith's argument, and the reason he receives so much adulation from conservatives, is his charge that all state intervention is counterproductive. Logically, if self-interest led to the common good, outside interference could only serve to compromise it. In this original version of "greed is good," the governor of self-interest becomes the market itself. If the butcher's self-interest gets the better of her, she will soon find that other butchers take away her business by underpricing her. The market, Smith reasoned in probably his most atavistic conclusion, even regulated the labour market. Research conducted in his native Scotland showed that a woman who mothered twelve children would be lucky to have one or two survive. This reflected the stark reality of a time when infant mortality—brought about by a combination of food shortages and disease—killed the majority of newborns before they had the opportunity to enter the labour market, even though they did so sometimes as young as age four. When wages increased (as was the case in Smith's time) families could afford to buy more food, meaning more children were likely to survive infancy. But as a larger number of children grew into workers and competed for jobs, they put downward pressure on wages, which translated into less money to buy food. This inevitably meant a return to a higher infant mortality rate, which resulted in fewer workers and higher wages, and so on. A rather cruel observation, but at the time an accurate one.

Smith, like Marx and the French sociologist Emile Durkheim, was also fascinated with the division of labour. Being the eternal optimist, Smith saw specialization as an integral component of wealth creation. *The Wealth* begins with an illustration of the wonders associated with the division of labour, a visit to a pin factory. Smith estimated that a single and untrained pin-maker working on his own could manufacture between one and twenty pins a day. But once the process was divided into discrete tasks—where "One draws out the wire, another straightens it, a third cuts it, a fourth points it . . ." and so on (up to eighteen different tasks were identified by Smith)—productivity increased phenomenally. Smith reported that in one factory he visited, ten workers (some performing more than one task) could produce 48 000 pins a day. This almost fantastic increase in productivity was solely due to the division of labour. From there, Smith urged specialization for everything and everybody, be it individuals, towns, even countries. Specialization would inevitably result in increases in productivity, which, in turn, would boost the overall amount of wealth for all involved. Taiwan, for example, should specialize in the production of oranges and trade them for Fuji apples from Japan. That way everybody is likely to get what he wants, and by specializing, no country wastes valuable resources producing what it is inept at in the first place. This reasoning, with only a few alterations contributed by David Ricardo, continues to provide the rationale for many of the arguments for free trade today.

Historical Perspective

In order to properly assess Smith's defence of free markets, one needs to understand the historical context in which he wrote. Smith is most often invoked by those critical of state interference, and to some extent those detractors are correct in ascribing to Smith a healthy mistrust of the state. But it is important to acknowledge that the state Smith wrote about was a vastly different animal from the state of today. At the time, there was no universal franchise and the average citizen had few political or even civil rights. Parliament was primarily controlled by wealthy property owners, many from aristocratic backgrounds, and a burgeoning merchant class. With no voters to answer to, these elites were able to run the state like a private business, solely for their personal gain and that of their friends and relatives. In this extreme version of cronyism, property, patronage, and power went hand in hand. While patronage continues to be a highly charged political issue today, the current system of nepotism pales in comparison with the abuse that went on in the eighteenth and nineteenth centuries. Karl Marx and his lifelong friend and collaborator Friedrich Engels summarized this system succinctly when they wrote that "The executive of the modern state is but a committee for managing the common affairs of the whole bourgeoisie."[17] In other words, the state was used by a well-connected elite to control the market solely for its own benefit. Consequently, few trusted the state and many, like Smith and later Marx, wanted to see its power drastically reduced or even abolished.[18]

Mercantilist practices put a lie to the commonly held belief that capitalist markets developed naturally over time. In stark contrast, markets were deliberately planned and implemented. The appropriation of territories in the "New World" involved a considerable amount of military force and other types of coercion, leaving virtually no room for laissez-faire. The British state, and by extension its wealthy elite, controlled every aspect of this process. Such efforts were not expended for the general level of wealth of the nation, as Smith would have wanted, but for the elite's own and immediate advantage. Smith railed against the state precisely for these reasons: the granting of monopolies by the state to a handful of companies solely for the benefit of that same state elite.

The case of the Hudson's Bay Company in Canada provides an instructive example of how closed these markets were. In 1670, Charles II granted the charter for the company to his cousin Prince Rupert. Bestowed along with the corporation, among other things, was a monopoly of trade in the region. This was no insignificant piece of real estate, but encompassed the area bounded by the rivers that flowed into Hudson Bay. Charles II also generously provided Prince Rupert with a seed fund of 110 000 pounds. Similarly, the English East India Company, established by Queen Elizabeth I in 1600, granted a monopoly of trade in Asia, Africa, and America. Other colonizing empires, such as the Dutch and the French, had similar arrangements. Not only did mercantilism translate into a monopoly of production, it also provided a captive market for British manufactured goods. In some instances it was illegal for the colonies, such as Canada, to compete with British industries, thus maintaining an impermeable market and no price competition for British goods. This patronage system not only extended to international trade, but also afflicted the domestic market. Within Great Britain, Parliament was stacked with wealthy landowners who successfully kept foreign competition at bay by imposing tariffs on grains. This situation lasted for centuries, and was not resolved until the middle of the nineteenth century.

In addition to practising what could only be considered forced trade—that is, total authority over both imports and exports—Great Britain tightly controlled the transportation of these goods. Under the Navigation Acts, British ships had a virtual monopoly on the transport of goods within the empire. (The only exception to this was products imported from outside the empire, which could be transported on ships owned by the country of origin.) These acts, first introduced in 1651 and modified many times throughout their nearly two-hundred-year existence (they were not repealed until 1849), also required that ships used for the transportation of goods had to be built within the British Empire. The acts even legislated who could work on these ships, stipulating that 75 percent of the crews had to be English. The Navigation Acts were continually tightened, and statutes such as the Woolens Act of 1699 and the Iron Act of 1750 prevented even the colonies from competing with Britain in those industries.

Furthermore, all products traded within the empire, no matter their destination, had to go through Great Britain where merchants were sure to take their share of the profits. For example, all North American tobacco destined for Europe went through British ports, three-quarters of which then went on to the rest of Europe. No foreign carriers could transport these goods, and no tobacco grown outside of the empire was allowed to compete. In short, the British elite had arranged quite a little deal for itself, with full control not only over all imports and exports but also their transportation. One should keep in mind that Great Britain greatly prospered from its tight grip on trade, the very antithesis of free trade. Far from impoverishing Great Britain, mercantilism helped it to establish itself as the wealthiest country on earth.

Mercantilist practices were successful in completely shifting the focus of international trade from the European continent to overseas. At the time that Smith wrote, more than half of Britain's trade was transcontinental (that is, not with Europe but other continents), which is a much higher proportion than today.[19] Many people benefited from this arrangement, including those who counted themselves among Smith's friends, the merchants of Glasgow. But counter to his friends' interests, Smith argued that Great Britain would benefit if it abandoned its nepotistic policies for the simple fact that they led to higher prices for the British consumer. From Smith's perspective, consumers had every reason to be pessimistic, as high tariffs on products such as cotton, leather, and silk kept prices artificially inflated. Smith reasoned the application of these duties particularly affected the poor by excluding them from the consumer market.

And so it went for much of British society: The well-being of the poorer classes was largely ignored. Many elites went so far as to argue that there was an unrecognized utility in poverty, in that it kept the poor desperate enough to work at subsistence wages. Increased costs were not the only reason to avoid higher wages. As was typical of the day, it was assumed that the poor lacked the moral fortitude to properly manage any extra income and were likely to splurge it on drink and other debauchery. Smith took issue with this rather condescending view and contended, a point that turned out to be another major theme of his book, that a higher level of consumption by the average worker would be rewarded with an increased level of wealth for the nation as a whole. In what might have appeared revolutionary at the time, and is seldom acknowledged by supporters of Smith today, he wrote that "No society can surely be flourishing and happy, of which the far greater part of the members are poor and miserable."[20]

In addition to monopolies and high tariffs, another development that kept markets from operating efficiently was the guilds. Powerful guilds convinced Parliament that they should be able to control the number of craftspeople working within their trades. Management of these numbers was regulated by restricting the number of apprentices entering the trade. As is the case with any monopoly, this resulted in workers being able to keep prices, and therefore wages, artificially high. These guilds, however, were already in steady decline throughout Smith's time and were finally abolished in the early nineteenth century.

Smith saw monopoly everywhere, and railed against it. He was particularly suspicious of the intentions of merchants and business people and wrote that "People of the same trade seldom meet together, even for merriment and diversion, but the conversation ends in a conspiracy against the public, or in some contrivance to raise prices."[21] Smith was equally suspicious of the emerging industrial classes "whose interest is never exactly the same with that of the public, who have generally an interest to deceive and even to oppress the public, and who accordingly have, upon many occasions, both deceived and oppressed it."[22]

Given his obvious distaste for monopolies, it is surprising that Smith downplayed the power of corporations. He famously referred to England as "a nation of shopkeepers," no doubt believing this characteristic would define British society well into the future. Despite monopolizing tendencies all around him, Smith felt that private corporations would fail because of misplaced self-interest. He feared this trait, which he considered to be integral to the working of the market, would become so diluted in a corporate structure that it would be rendered useless. Since corporations involved the administration of other people's money, their managers would not watch over others' finances "with the same anxious vigilance" that they would their own. Consequently, corporations, he reasoned, would be unable to compete with self-owned enterprises. Yet Great Britain quickly evolved from the nation of shopkeepers that Smith observed, and seventy-two years later Marx and Engels wrote that "Modern industry has converted the little workshop . . . into the great factory of the industrial capitalist."[23] In that sense, Marx and Engels more accurately predicted the rise of the modern corporation, which would forever change the landscape of capitalism. Smith also greatly underestimated the full impact of the Industrial Revolution. The technology that undergirded so many changes in modern society—factories, mass production, urbanization—had either not yet been invented, or was in little use. To this topic we will turn next.

Poverty and the Industrial Revolution

Even those only remotely familiar with the work of Adam Smith are aware that his was a rather positive assessment of capitalism. In stark contrast, Marx was critical of the tumult that was the Industrial Revolution and of free markets in general, and likewise, it is Marx's name that first comes to mind when considering the dark side of capitalism. So divergent were Smith's and Marx's interpretations, it makes one wonder whether the two were actually writing about the same planet, let alone the same country. In fact, the two were separated by only a few hundred miles and scarcely more than a half century. One could easily trace these differences in evaluation to temperament, to an inherent optimism or pessimism. But this answer would not be satisfying, for it would ignore the profound changes that British society underwent in the time separating the two social theorists.

Counter to the image of the economist as practitioner of the dismal science, Smith was the eternal optimist. And Smith had good reason to be optimistic, for economic circumstances in the late eighteenth century looked quite promising. Whether one pegs the beginning of the Industrial Revolution at 1760 or 1780, Smith wrote *The Wealth* either in the revolution's early stages or before it had even begun. With the exception of Charles Watt's steam engine, Smith fails to mention any technological advances; his focus was the specialization that grew out of the division of labour. In any case, the future looked bright for the inhabitants of Great Britain in the second half of the eighteenth century, even for the poor. Feudal relations were abolished in 1740, and advances in agriculture meant poor harvests no longer resulted in starvation. For the first time, the wages of a day labourer were enough to support a family, albeit at a subsistence level. Labourers engaged in such "luxuries" as tea, and for the first time in history, were able to participate in the consumer market. Wages rose particularly quickly in the two decades that preceded the publication of *The Wealth*. People were also living longer and the death rate plummeted markedly. The plague had been eradicated for over a century, and other diseases such as typhus and smallpox were in decline. In short, Great Britain was still primarily a rural society, and the more gloomy aspects of the Industrial and capitalist revolutions were still in retreat.

In 1848, seven decades after *The Wealth* was first published, Marx and Engels wrote the *Manifesto of the Communist Party*. By then economic conditions in Great Britain had changed profoundly, and Smith's optimism was replaced by Marx's pessimism. Rapid advances in productivity had been achieved thanks to industrialization, but these gains were not shared with workers as Smith had urged. Quite the contrary, the well-being of the average worker had declined dramatically. While the death rate had experienced a secular decline between 1780 and 1810, this development did not last. Around the middle of the nineteenth century, when Marx and Engels mounted their scathing critique of capitalism, the death rate in Great Britain was once again on the rise. This reversal could be traced to a number of factors, such as an increase in disease, including consumption (tuberculosis) and cholera, as well as industrial accidents. This was particularly evident in the urban centres, where a lack of sanitation combined with ignorance provided a fertile environment for the spread of disease. Dirty water, open sewers, and crowded living conditions encouraged disease to thrive. The contrast between the newly emerging urban centres and the old rural way of life could not have been starker. In 1840, in the rural district of Rutlandshire, the average age of death for a tradesman was forty-one. In Liverpool, it was almost half that at twenty-two. Labourers fared even worse, the average age of death being fifteen in the city compared with thirty-eight in the rural areas. This divide even affected the gentry, the average age of death being only thirty-five in Liverpool compared with fifty-two in the country.[24]

Whatever the reason—be it capitalism, industrialization, or urbanization—one could no longer take such a sanguine view of the developments that slowly, but forcefully, transformed British society. Although Marx and Engels might have put a decidedly pessimistic spin on it, there was little to be positive about in mid-nineteenth-century Great Britain. This was particularly true for those who lived in cities, and even more so for the poor. The Industrial Revolution not only transformed Great Britain, but also slowly spread to the Continent and eventually to other parts of the world. What has not changed is that free markets continue to have both their adherents and detractors. And while it is the wealthy who continue to promulgate the ideas of Adam Smith, poor people around the world are inspired by the writings of Marx and Engels. In that, Smith was right: People know where their interests lie.

The Act of Settlement

Another piece of legislation that impeded free markets during Smith's time were a series of restrictions placed on the movement of people within Great Britain, which, not surprisingly, applied only to the poor. As mentioned, the elites thought quite ill of the poor and were under the impression that they required extensive guidance. This included a general concern that the unhindered movement of the lower classes could only result in chaos and social disorder. This distrust found its legal formation in the Act of Settlement. But before we look at this act in detail, some background is in order. In 1831, there were 15 500 parishes in England and Wales, each being responsible for the supervision of its own poor.[25] Revenues were generated in a variety of ways, all of which ended up taxing local landowners. As one would expect, there was considerable variation in wealth among these parishes, and consequently in the generosity of their payouts.

At the heart of the problem was that the poor, self-interested creatures that they were, naturally gravitated towards the more generous parishes. Although competition was generally seen in a positive light, this particular kind was not, as it placed an undue financial burden on the more charitable parishes. As one would expect, the number of poor quickly increased or decreased in direct relation to the amount of relief paid. In order to nip this particular market mechanism in the bud, British Parliament introduced the Act of Settlement (sometimes referred to as the Laws of Settlement), which limited migration of the poor within Great Britain. In combination with the Poor Laws of 1601, the Act of Settlement, introduced in 1662, provided the foundation for poor relief (the equivalent of social assistance today) and mandated that the poor be registered in their home parish. In order to check migration, the poor were allowed to collect alms in their home parish only and could not settle and collect payment in another. Additionally, if paupers left their home parish without permission, they were not allowed to return and resume collecting at a later date.

While on the surface this sounded like an adequate solution, the unintended consequence of this legislation was that it impeded the flow of labour. Workers, understandably, were reluctant to leave their home parish, even if work was available elsewhere. Given that there was no guarantee they could return to their original parish once they became unemployed again, this decision was only rational. Furthermore, the poor were also prohibited from collecting alms in the new parish because they were not registered. Many commentators felt this whole arrangement was rather nonsensical and argued against these laws on the basis that they obstructed the proper orchestration of the labour market. The irrational result of this seemingly rational legislation was that whereas one parish might have plenty of work, but no workers, another might have plenty of workers, but no work. The lifting of the Act of Settlement, which did not occur until 1834, was an obvious solution to this impediment of the labour market.[26] Although it seems antiquated, this law is actually still applied today, the only exception being that the jurisdiction has changed from the parish to the nation state.

Smith Today

Given Smith's continued popularity, it is worthwhile asking how applicable his writings are today. First, a proviso. Poverty and economic wealth are relative terms. Smith lived at a time when material wealth was growing rapidly, and by that standard, he had good reason to be hopeful. At the same time, let us not forget that Smith was a person of some privilege and did not suffer from the same privation that the majority of Britons did. As he himself pointed out, infant mortality was astoundingly high, particularly by contemporary standards, and the kind of poverty then experienced by the average labourer is probably unimaginable by today's standards, at least in the West. These hardships were partly due to a lack of medical facilities and knowledge, but, as Smith reveals in his analysis of the labour market, many children failed to survive for want of food. One could say, to be diplomatic about it, that Smith was a bit insensitive about the whole thing. Furthermore, throughout Smith's life considerable changes were taking their toll on the poor. The privatization of land, and the enclosures of communal land previously used for common grazing, caused adversity for many. Hundreds of thousands of people in Great Britain became unemployed and roamed the countryside and towns. In other words, even as conditions were improving, Smith might have wilfully ignored some of the less appealing developments of his time.

In any case, Smith very much lived in the calm before the storm that was the Industrial Revolution and to him late-eighteenth-century Great Britain appeared, and probably was, quite the tranquil place, although, as he argued so cogently, capable of improvement. The free market, as Smith envisioned it, was conceived to be an effective defence against all kinds of monopoly: the planned markets of the mercantilist system; the conspiracy to control prices by tradespeople and industrialists; and the impediments to a free labour market, borders artificially erected by parishes afraid of an onslaught of the poor.

The fact that he never anticipated the Industrial Revolution, or the rise of monopoly capitalism, puts in doubt the utility of some of his observations to contemporary circumstances. Smith would no doubt be surprised to see the degree to which the world now caters to the consumer. The choice and abundance available even to the average worker is simply astounding by historical standards. Given his position that the best yardstick for the measurement of wealth was the living standards of the average worker, Smith would likely be impressed by conditions in the West, but critical of the huge differences in wealth that endure between the First and the Third worlds. Most antiquated are his thoughts about how competition alone can effectively regulate the supply of workers. Few children, at least in the West, die before they reach adulthood, and natural checks such as disease and starvation no longer exist to regulate the labour market. For a variety of reasons, the supply of labour does not always match its demand, and periods of mass unemployment have plagued labour markets in the past two centuries. Again, Marx and Engels took a different position and condemned the presence of what they called an army of the unemployed, which was effectively used to keep wages down.

Smith would, no doubt, be surprised at the power of corporations and, likely, given his position on monopolies in general, would be highly critical of them. His Britain was one of small shopkeepers, where individual capitalists were on relatively equal footing with one another. "Small" is the operative word here, for at the time business still played a minor economic role. To be sure, there were powerful economic actors such as wealthy landowners who had strong ties to Parliament. But it was precisely this system of patronage that Smith argued should be dismantled, anticipating its dissolution would lead to what is now often referred to as a "level playing field." Although the system of mercantilism was gradually dismantled not long after Smith's death, contemporary critics of free trade argue that the power vacuum left by wealthy landowners and powerful merchants was simply taken up by corporations, for it is these behemoths that now dictate to the state what policies to enact.

Modern economies have evolved considerably since Smith first reflected on these issues in *The Wealth*, and trade now occurs in a world that is increasingly post-industrial; a world no longer the province of small shopkeepers but of multinational corporations. With an eye to history, some economists have applied Smith's critique of mercantilism to contemporary circumstances, tellingly referring to these relationships as neo-mercantilism. They argue that powerful industries are now able to win protection from open markets in much the same manner that merchants were able to do in Smith's day, be it through tariffs, subsidies, or patent protection. The pharmaceutical industry lobbying for worldwide patents, for example, is tantamount to monopolization. But it cleverly asks for these provisions under the guise of free trade. In other words, little has changed; mercantilism lives but is now called free trade.

Demonstrators against free trade have more or less adopted this position. They argue we have failed to transcend the cozy relationships between wealth and political power that defined mercantilism. Instead of landed aristocrats and wealthy landowners, there are now large corporations that use governments to force their way. Critics charge that the recent string of free trade agreements are the direct result of intensive lobbying by corporations, who have succeeded in convincing governments to take up their cause. Marx and Engels acknowledged this relationship long ago when they observed that "[The bourgeoisie] has set up that single, unconscionable freedom—Free Trade."[27] While those who oppose free trade often find guidance in the work of Marx and Engels, supporters usually find their inspiration in Smith. But upon closer inspection, Marx and Smith have far more in common than their respective admirers realize. Both railed against the abuse of power and privilege of their day; both sought the decentralization of power; both argued for more democracy; both celebrated and expressed confidence in individual freedom. Unfortunately, economic conservatives of the day have distorted and misinterpreted Smith's work to the point of caricature. They forget that Smith was not an uncritical supporter of free markets, and that he was just as concerned about the welfare of the average worker as that of the capitalist.

Whereas Smith is invoked to defend free markets in general, Ricardo is best known for mobilizing a defence of free trade. It is his work that we will discuss next.

3

DAVID RICARDO: SO WHAT DOES THAT HAVE TO DO WITH THE PRICE OF CORN IN ENGLAND?

DAVID RICARDO'S THEORY of comparative advantage was directly informed by events that led to the introduction of free trade in the British Empire. But how far are we able to generalize from this particular incident; that is, does Ricardo's argument for free trade hold true for all times and places? This is no trivial matter, for Ricardo's theory of comparative advantage underpins the mandate of institutions like the WTO and provides the intellectual foundation for all modern free trade agreements. For this reason, we need to look at his theory in some detail.

David Ricardo was born in 1772 in London, England, and wrote primarily in the first quarter of the nineteenth century. During the half century that separates the work of Ricardo and Smith, the British political and economic scene had changed significantly. Ricardo's observations were made at a time when the Industrial Revolution was in full bloom and Great Britain was well on its way to becoming the first urban society. In the 1770s, when Smith was writing *The Wealth*, half of Britain's population earned its livelihood from farming; around Ricardo's time, this proportion had fallen to one-third. Another characteristic that distinguished Smith's and Ricardo's ages was technology. As we saw, Smith traced the remarkable increases in productivity to the division of labour, the crucial point being that these tasks were still performed by human hands.[28] By Ricardo's time, this process had evolved and machines were increasingly replacing the work once done by humans. To distinguish between these two methods of production, a separation is commonly drawn between the age of manufactory and that of industry.

The age of industry changed society so profoundly that Smith could not even have imagined it only a half century hence. By the time Ricardo was writing, the Industrial Revolution had arrived with full force and Britain was no longer a "nation of shopkeepers," as Smith had so quaintly described it. The decisive event that provided the basis for Ricardo's fame, however, had little to do with the Industrial Revolution or technology, and everything to do with a fight over a piece of legislation known as the Corn Laws. Centuries old, these laws protected local farmers from foreign competition by placing tariffs on imported grain. And it was the abolition of these laws that would occupy a considerable portion of Ricardo's life, making him famous in the process.

The Corn Laws

The Corn Laws proved to be the central event in the battle over free trade in mid-nineteenth-century Great Britain. These laws, in place in Great Britain under various guises since 1436, consisted of a sliding scale of tariffs designed to regulate the importation of corn (the British term for grain). Not everyone agreed these laws were beneficial, particularly those forced to pay higher prices for bread. This controversy came to a head around the turn of the nineteenth century, when a quickly growing population led to an increased demand for grain. At the same time, a series of bad crops translated into a dwindling supply. And as every first-year economics student well knows, when increased demand and decreased supply meet, the result is higher prices. In retrospect, the obvious solution was to lower tariffs and welcome cheaper grain from abroad. But powerful landowners pressured the British Parliament into keeping foreign grain from coming into the country, as they feared cheap imports would lower the price of land. Of particular concern to British landowners was competition from the recently independent United States, with its huge tracts of fertile land. Given the close ties between landowners and Parliament—often they were one and the same—landowners were not only successful in keeping the tariffs in place but even raising them. Due to ever-increasing tariffs, the price of corn followed a slow but steady upward trend. Between 1770 and 1810, the price of corn more than doubled. In 1815, the law was further amended and outright prohibited the importation of wheat if and when the price of wheat in Britain went below 80 shillings.[29] But no sooner did it look as though the situation was getting out of hand than things took a turn for the better and some of the pressures that had pushed up prices lost their force. The defeat of Napoleon, in addition to a return of good harvests, signalled a drop in prices, and the issue lost some of its urgency.

That same year, 1815, Ricardo published a pamphlet entitled "Essay on the Influence of a Low Price of Corn on the Profits of Stock," in which he argued that the high price of corn meant higher prices for land, and not the other way around. Given what his adherents are saying today, it is interesting to note that he argued for "a substantially free trade in corn" and not complete free trade, nor for all products. He further argued that Great Britain would greatly benefit by giving up agriculture altogether and specializing in the export of manufactured goods. Thus he hit upon the doctrine of comparative advantage. Encouraged by his good friend James Mill, Ricardo elaborated on the ideas first laid out in his pamphlet, resulting in his best-known work, *The Principles of Political Economy and Taxation* (1817). The success of his pamphleteering convinced Ricardo to join Parliament, which meant, for all intents and purposes, buying a seat. In his case, it entailed providing an interest-free loan of 25 000 British pounds to the overseer of a small riding in Ireland, a riding Ricardo never even visited. He "won" the seat in 1819 and held it until his death in 1823. But even from the inside, Ricardo was unable to convince Parliament to rescind the Corn Laws.

Ricardo, like his predecessor Smith, took into consideration a variety of interests, particularly those of landowners and industrialists. While the high price of corn did benefit landowners, it worked out to the disadvantage of nearly everyone else. Particularly hard hit were manufacturers, who, at a time when wages trailed the price of bread, were burdened with higher overheads. Ricardo defended the burgeoning industrialists, and argued that all their profits were effectively skimmed by landowners, as higher prices for bread resulted in higher rents for land. This extra burden, Ricardo felt, inhibited the proper development of productive forces and slowed industrial development. One cannot accuse Ricardo of making this argument out of self-interest. Despite being a wealthy landowner himself, Ricardo sided with the manufacturing class on this issue. Although he admitted that landowners would be hurt initially, he projected that lower food prices would benefit Great Britain in the long run. In addition to lower wages, manufacturers would further benefit from the importation of grain by providing foreign consumers with British pounds, which could then, in turn, be used to buy British manufactured goods.

Ricardo was not alone in his opposition to the Corn Laws. A series of petitions signed by merchants, calling for the termination of tariffs on corn, was sent to Parliament, most notably in 1820 and 1822. By 1839, workers, farmers who leased from the landowners, and merchants organized around the Anti–Corn League, but to no avail. Change did come about, but it would be a long time coming. It was not until the depression of 1839 that the British government finally considered some of the arguments in favour of free trade. Six years later, in 1845, tariffs on grain were drastically reduced (although tariffs remained on many other products, including cotton, wine, sugar, tea, and rum). And it was not until 1846 that the Corn Laws were officially repealed and replaced by free trade. Unfortunately, Ricardo did not live to see the day, for by that time he had already been dead for nearly a quarter century.

As we just saw, various developments contributed to the dismantling of the Corn Laws. The demands of the Napoleonic Wars and a string of bad harvests conspired to increase the price of corn far beyond what could be considered reasonable. An already dire situation was further exacerbated by the fact that an easy solution lay at hand: Most people were aware that cheap corn from abroad could have easily managed the crises. But change came about only as the dynamics of the political landscape shifted. Increased industrialization slowly undermined the power of the landowners, and over a span of only a few decades, agriculture ceased to be the main engine of economic growth in Great Britain. In that sense, the abrogation of the Corn Laws symbolized the dwindling influence of landowners and the ascendancy of the manufacturing class.

Comparative Advantage

In the seventeenth century, people believed that God endowed each individual with a particular talent, making each and every one naturally adept at some task. Using similar logic, political economists put forward the idea that countries also had certain aptitudes, and argued they should engage in the production of goods at which they were naturally superior. Canada and Russia have plenty of trees, for example, and it is only logical that they should exploit this resource and trade lumber on the world market. In economics this is referred to as absolute advantage; a country does whatever it is best at.

But the astute reader will wonder what happens if a country, or a person for that matter, lacks an absolute advantage. To put it bluntly, what is in store for a country that is not superior at anything and lacks any and all absolute advantages? Is such a country forced to retreat from economic life?

A cogent answer to this question would not appear until David Ricardo wrote about comparative advantage in *The Principles of Political Economy*. This theory, and it is important to recognize that it is just a theory, stipulates that it is less important what a country is best at than what it is comparatively good at. Ricardo's insight was that "under free trade, each country will find it profitable to export not just those goods that it can produce more cheaply than other countries, but also goods that it can produce more cheaply compared with the goods it imports; even when it produces everything more expensively than anyone else, there are still benefits to be obtained from international trade, not just for the country in question, but for all countries taken together."[30] As Herman Daly and John Cobb observe, "The pure logic of comparative advantage, within the world of its assumptions, is unassailable."[31] So rather than go into technical detail about the model itself, our time is better spent examining some of the assumptions that Daly and Cobb allude to.

The first of these assumptions is that there is no unemployment. To illustrate his argument, Ricardo provides an example of two countries, England and Portugal, both of which produce cloth and wine, with Portugal having an absolute advantage in the production of both. Although things do not look good for England, Ricardo goes on to argue that through comparative advantage both will gain.[32] But his argument very much hinges on how much work there is available, or to put it slightly differently, he assumes full employment. If Portugal has the wine market all tied up and enough additional resources (labour and capital) at its disposal, there is nothing to stop it from dominating the cloth market, too. It can, after all, out-perform England in both activities. In the real world this is exactly how such scenarios unfold. In other words, Ricardo's model assumes there is enough work for all to go around. But this is no longer the case in a world plagued by high unemployment and overproduction. There are currently around 30 million unemployed workers in the West alone, and any country that did not fight to keep its jobs would quickly find itself with a bigger share of the world's unemployed.

Second, as Daly and Cobb point out, Ricardo did not expect capital to be mobile. If Portugal had cheaper labour and better growing conditions, an English firm might well relocate to Portugal and grow its wine there. Since this would entail using Portuguese labour, it would be of little advantage to England (other than to the consumer). Third, the unit of analysis in Ricardo's example is countries, England and Portugal. But the fact is, then as now, that private producers decide what to manufacture and not governments. Thus, a pact in which one country focuses its energies on cloth and another on wine would be difficult, if not impossible, to enforce. The fact is that individual manufacturers produce anything they can. Let's say that Japan has both an absolute and comparative advantage in manufacturing cars. According to Ricardo's theory, competing countries should then be happy to give up production in that area and focus on whatever other activity they are good at. For whatever reason, most countries have neglected to use Ricardo's advice, and conse-quently Germany, Korea, the United States, Italy, Great

Britain, Sweden, and France, among others, continue to produce automobiles. This behaviour is replicated in almost every other industry, and we find countries throughout the world producing things at which they have neither an absolute nor a comparative advantage.

It is also important to keep in mind that the world economy is a much different place than it was in Ricardo's day. Let us review some of the unique characteristics of his case study, Great Britain. Based on the urging of Ricardo and an assortment of farmers, merchants, and industrialists, free trade was eventually adopted and proved to be a relative success for Great Britain.[33] Great Britain was fortunate in that it could boast superiority in a number of areas, which greatly facilitated its transition to a free trade regime. Primary among those was its technological advantage, which translated into little to no competition from the rest of the world. These advantages, however, would soon be challenged by other countries, in particular Germany and the United States, who were also industrializing. At first, this competition had little effect on the British economy, as there was enough demand around the world for industrial products to allow for more than one producer. But this has changed drastically over the course of the past century and a half. Since most First World countries are now on a relative equal footing as far as technology is concerned, technological superiority does not automatically translate into big wins any more. All industrial economies are capable of producing the majority of goods their consumers desire: automobiles, furniture, appliances. The seemingly unlimited market for manufactured products that lay ahead of Great Britain in the middle of the nineteenth century has vanished and been replaced by a saturated one.

A seldom-acknowledged downside associated with comparative advantage is that once a country specializes in a product and its market weakens or disappears, there is usually no other market to replace it. Canada has often been criticized for relying too much on what it is naturally good at, resource extraction. Once there is a downturn in one of these industries, as has happened with fish and coal, whole regions are affected. That alone is a good argument for diversification of the economy, not specialization. Furthermore, once a country specializes to the point of having driven out all competitors, it has a monopoly. Any advantages that are calculated to accrue to other players because of specialization immediately vanish once monopolies enter the picture. According to the theory, this is unlikely to cause much harm, for as soon as monopolies do develop, other producers are supposed to step in and drive prices down again. Easy in theory, more difficult in practice: Once a local car, airline, or wheat industry is gone, it can be difficult to re-establish.

At the heart of the issue is how much faith we are willing to put in the market. If the auto industry encountered a slump, should Canada stand by and let the industry perish? Economic planning might be called for, but unfortunately, an industrial policy usually involves subsidies, which are strictly forbidden by the WTO. The free market solution is to seek out another industry, but this advice is a bit hard to swallow given that most profitable industries are already spoken for: the aerospace industry, automobiles, computer technology, pharmaceuticals. Any government that allowed industries to fail in order to exploit its comparative advantage would quickly be producing very little. If the United States abandoned its auto industry, Japan could easily increase production to compensate for that loss. And what would the United States do—focus its production on computers? Well, that market is saturated, too. In any case, it is unlikely that there would be enough jobs in the computer industry to recoup those lost in the automobile industry. The fact is that countries do not adhere to the rules of comparative advantage and intervene in the economy at every opportunity. One of the most lucrative industries in the world, the automobile industry, is generously subsidized and includes training grants, loans, duty remissions, tax abatement grants, infrastructure, and more.[34] Furthermore, firms demand subsidies up front as the following headline in *The Globe and Mail* illustrates: "Ford warns: Subsidize or lose jobs."[35] Such threats are unfortunately not without merit, and a country that decides to ignore them because they go counter to the rules of free trade will do so at its own peril.

One should keep in mind that Ricardo sided with the burgeoning industrialists, whose interests at the time were subordinated to those of landowners. But times have changed, and industrialists are no longer discriminated against. And while both Ricardo and Smith touched upon the interests of the worker, these concerns are mostly forgotten in contemporary accounts. Ricardo, like Smith, railed against the dominating influence that landowners had over Parliament. This domination has now been replaced by that of industrialists and it is doubtful that Ricardo, or for that matter, Smith, would stand up to defend the interests of the contemporary corporate elites.

Even if the tariffs that Great Britain applied to foreign corn hurt the average consumer of the day, it does not automatically follow that all tariffs are equally bad. If the market is flooded with wine from England, and Portugal introduces a tariff because it wants to protect its own industry, does this always have to be assessed in a negative light? Is it not better to give an ailing industry a lending hand for a year or two rather than risk losing it altogether? Chrysler and Volkswagen both experienced some bad years that required financial aid from their respective governments, and both recuperated sufficiently to become competitive once again. The alternative, allowing them to fail, would not have been, in retrospect, that wise of a decision.

And last, if free trade is so obviously beneficial to all countries involved, why do we need so many agreements and regulations to enforce it? Maybe this is because its benefits are less obvious than we are led to believe. Maybe, even, non-existent. Given such doubts, countries are reluctant to let well-established industries expire. If comparative advantage were as beneficial as its proponents claim, why do governments over and again intervene in their economies in order to protect, attract, and establish industries? And why do industries clamour for protection and demand subsidies? If a country refuses to participate in the riches that are supposed to flow from free trade, why not let it suffer in inevitable poverty and have everybody learn an important lesson? If a country insists on wasting its taxes on helping industries, does this not benefit consumers elsewhere? Why spend so much time and energy convincing everybody that free trade is so beneficial? Maybe because it is not.

Friedrich List

No history of free trade can be considered complete without at least a mention of a contemporary of Ricardo's, the German academic Friedrich List (1789–1846). List also supported free trade and advocated a commercial union among the German-speaking states shortly after the close of the Napoleonic Wars. This position was so unpopular that he was charged with sedition and put in jail in 1824. Released the following year, he moved to the United States, only to return to Germany in 1832. It seems that his once-radical ideas quickly transformed into the acceptable, and a German customs union was put into place over a six-year period starting in 1828, only a few short years after List was jailed for first suggesting the very same thing.

So far it seems that List was the German counterpart of Ricardo, someone who courageously championed free trade at a time when few did. But this is where the similarities end. List's support for free trade was not unqualified and he added some important provisos. He proposed that countries should make use of tariffs, as well as subsidies, to help them develop fledgling industries. Without such assistance, he argued, burgeoning industries would be unable to compete with already established firms abroad. His book *The National System of Political Economy*, published in 1841, was specifically aimed at Germany in the early stages of industrialization. This was also about the time, five years previous to be precise, that Great Britain abolished its Corn Laws. But not all countries emulated Britain's policy of free trade, and for a variety of reasons some chose to follow the advice of List and others like him. List's ideas were directly adopted in Japan and elsewhere in Asia. Other economists throughout history have argued against free trade, some of them quite successfully. In the 1820s, under the urging of Senator Henry Clay, the United States introduced tariffs to protect its industries, a policy known as the American System. Other prominent Americans who argued for protectionism were the newspaper editor and publisher Mathew Carey and his son, the economist Henry Carey. But it seems this side of the debate has suffocated under an avalanche of pro–free trade arguments and is seldom heard.

List's work merits attention because it provides another version of the free trade story. Historically, the major industrial powers—Germany, the United States, Japan, and Great Britain before that—all coddled their industries in a very protective environment before sending them off to compete in the world economy. None of these countries became an economic powerhouse through free trade and they only adopted this stance once their industries were already competitive. Today, organizations like the WTO and World Bank urge Third World countries to embrace free trade without ever having enjoyed the benefits that come with protectionism and that are so important to cultivating domestic industries.

While the influence of the classical economists continues to loom large in today's economies, we have moved significantly beyond the free markets that were espoused by Smith and Ricardo. In today's advanced economies governments intervene in a multitude of ways. While there are many reasons for this, much of the intellectual groundwork for this change in the economy was provided by John Maynard Keynes, the subject of the following chapter.

4

The ideas of economists and political philosophers, both
when they are right and when they are wrong, are more
powerful than is commonly understood. Indeed, the world
is ruled by little else.
—JOHN MAYNARD KEYNES

JOHN MAYNARD KEYNES: CHALLENGING THE CLASSICAL ECONOMISTS

JOHN MAYNARD KEYNES (1883–1946) is significant because he challenged some of the basic tenets of the market as espoused by the two economists we just met, Adam Smith and David Ricardo. Keynes forcefully argued that the key assumptions about the free market made by his famous predecessors were just that, assumptions. Historically Keynes's writings are also relevant because they successfully bridged the rival ideologies of the nineteenth century: capitalism and socialism. Not only did Keynesian policies apply a much-needed brake to a sometimes out-of-control capitalism, they also provided an opportunity for a "middle way" in a world that was ideologically and politically divided between socialism and capitalism. Social democratic parties, such as the Sozialdemokratische Partei (SPD) in Germany and the New Democratic Party (NDP) in Canada, are a direct result of this compromise. But Keynes's influence went far beyond social democratic parties and affected all industrial countries. His influence has been so wide-ranging that former US president Richard Nixon, not a social democrat by any stretch of the imagination, was forced to admit in the 1970s that "We are all Keynesians now."

Some people would argue that Nixon's quote was made just as Keynes's influence was beginning to wane and that we have since witnessed a resurrection of the ideas of Smith and Ricardo. Particularly in this age of neo-liberalism, there appears to be little room for anyone who advocates state intervention of any kind. But to reject Keynes would be a mistake. Too often those who repudiate Keynes do so more out of wishful thinking than careful observation. The return to free markets has been met with only a modicum of success, and the state continues to play a significant role in all Western economies. As we shall find out, reports of the death of Keynesianism are greatly exaggerated. The mixed market continues to reign supreme not only in domestic economies but also in the international one. The most challenging part of this, it appears, is to get governments to admit it.

Keynes is best known for his writings on the Depression and for proposing what were, at least at the time, some unorthodox solutions. For this reason, it may seem odd to include him in a book on trade. But Keynes is important for our present purposes for three reasons. First, Keynes is the intellectual who provides legitimacy to state intervention, at least at the national level.

And what is beneficial at the national level, it will be argued, is also desirable at the international one. Today all industrial economies continue to practise some form of mixed economy (free market with some government intervention). None are completely free market, and the presence of Keynes continues to loom large in all Western economies. Free trade is difficult to enforce in an environment where governments routinely intervene in their economies. Second, and relatedly, it is somewhat hypocritical for international organizations like the World Bank to demand that Third World countries practise laissez-faire while there is so much state intervention in the First World. And third, Keynes had some important insights about the peace settlement imposed on Germany following the First World War. The lesson to be learned from that episode is that international co-operation and intervention can be used constructively, and there is no reason to believe that similar programs could not be used with equal success in the Third World. The only thing that seems to be missing is the political will.

The notion that government continues to play an important role in the economy may rankle some people, and may seem outright false to others. The fact, however, is that a large proportion of the GDP of industrial countries, from one-third to over half, continues to be channelled through government coffers. Even the United States, which has the most self-hating government on earth, spends one-third of its GDP on government services. And this is precisely why recessions—such as those in the 1980s, 1990s, and in 2001—have been less severe than they would have been otherwise, the simple reason being that government spending has kept the economy from further collapsing into a depression. A steady income for workers in education and health, the military, and other government sectors directly provides consumers with money to spend, which benefits the economy as a whole. In that sense, Keynes's ideas were, and continue to be, an effective antidote to the free market ideas espoused by so many contemporary politicians and economists. Governments may talk the free market talk, but they continue to have a considerable grip on domestic economies, and by extension, the international one.

With the advent of neo-liberalism and neo-conservatism in recent decades—Margaret Thatcher, Ronald Reagan, and Brian Mulroney—it may be surprising that government spending has decreased little, even in the past decade. Certainly, it continues to be much higher now than it was in the pre–Second World War era, and even higher than in the 1950s, 1960s, or even 1970s. Spending has been cut, and the growth of social programs has decelerated, but deceleration is not the same thing as a reversal, and in that sense, we have not experienced a watershed change in the way that economies have been run in the past half century. The most accurate description of government spending is that it has plateaued. So while governments openly espouse theories of free trade and unfettered markets, they are compelled to practise the tenets of Keynesianism because of political pressures. Why this is so is a complicated question. The answer may be attributed to the fact that any politician who actually dared to dismantle these programs to any serious degree would be committing political suicide. Imagine, for example, having to pay full tuition fees for elementary and secondary schools; or depending on the private sector to fund roads and bridges. Or having only private food inspection or police. What is more, the introduction of large-scale cuts is difficult to implement and even anti-state ideologues, such as Thatcher, Reagan, and Mulroney, have been exceedingly unsuccessful in slowing government spending. These politicians found out that once ideology meets reality, more practical considerations win out, and the status quo stubbornly endures.

Another reason to include Keynes in a book on trade is that he was one of, if not the, major architect of the post-war economy, which includes institutions like the World Bank and the IMF. Along with the WTO, these institutions play a central role in the current international order, and it is worthwhile, for this reason alone, to know more about the man. The fact that these institutions continue to thrive indicates that even conservatives admit, albeit tacitly, that international planning and intervention is necessary, or at least desirable, at some level. As we have already seen in the case of Great Britain in the eighteenth century, free markets did not just come about on their own, but were planned, managed, and manipulated. In much the same way, the World Bank, the IMF, and the WTO are constantly attempting to make other countries more market friendly, proving once again that, in the words of Karl Polyani, laissez-faire is planned.[36]

The Depression

Like Adam Smith and David Ricardo, John Maynard Keynes was born in and lived in Great Britain. And again like his predecessors, Keynes was a product of his time. His reputation, too, can be directly linked to a seminal event in world history: for Keynes, it was clearly the Depression of the 1930s. But unlike Smith and Ricardo, Keynes could have come from anywhere. Smith and Ricardo wrote about events that were, if not unique to, at least much further developed in Great Britain than elsewhere. The protracted revolution that accelerated the dominance of both markets and industrial production first took hold in Great Britain, and it is logical that its first commentators should also have hailed from there. The Depression, however, differed from these events in that it affected the whole of the industrialized world concurrently. Put another way, while the chronology of the Depression was of utmost importance to the development of Keynes's ideas, the fact that he came from Great Britain was somewhat inconsequential. Still, Keynes's fame rested on the fact that he came from a country whose government was tolerated both politically and intellectually, a country that was pro–free market and part of what would soon be the Allied powers. Germany, for example, had neither the requisite power nor the intellectual credibility. The candidate could equally likely have come from the United State or Sweden, as in both those countries similar ideas were already circulating. But it was Keynes who most cogently and persuasively presented these ideas. And fortunately for Keynes, Great Britain had both the respectability and economic prowess necessary to underwrite such an economist.

Keynes, however, was not the first to challenge the doctrines of laissez-faire. A string of economists and social commentators questioned the rationale underlying capitalism from its very beginnings. Free markets inspired trenchant critiques from a succession of brilliant minds. The authors included anarchists such as Pierre Joseph Proudhon and Charles Fourier, socialists such as Robert Owen, and communists such as Marx and Engels. But these critiques were unabashedly anti–free market and their goal was to displace the present system, not to reform it. Such radical ideas found little legitimacy in the West and some countries, including Canada, went to considerable lengths to crush movements openly hostile to free markets. Keynes needed to be careful when he negotiated these sensitive political waters, mindful not to upset those who were suspicious of anything that even insinuated socialism. As an academic he was compelled to acknowledge socialist thought; as a politician it would have been folly. Keynes had to be free market friendly—and there is little doubt that he was—in order for his ideas to gain acceptance among the political and economic elite. In that sense, Keynes saved the day, for not only could his solutions be implemented within a capitalist framework but also, he was, after all, one of "them," an ardent supporter of the market economy. Keynes's brilliant tactic, more than anything, lay in the fact that he was able to offer an alternative that did not disrupt the status quo and his ideas were revolutionary only in the sense that they did not compromise the integrity of the capitalist system.

The Treaty of Versailles and the German War Debt

During the First World War, Keynes worked for the British treasury. There he was involved in the peace negotiations following the war, which eventually resulted in the Treaty of Versailles. Unhappy with the direction these negotiations were taking, Keynes resigned. But he did not stop there and openly criticized the terms of the agreement in his essay *The Economic Consequences of Peace*, published in 1919. This book was the beginning of a preoccupation with international politics, a subject that would occupy Keynes's mind for the remainder of his life. In *The Economic Consequences*, Keynes criticized the punishing reparation payments that Germany was forced to endure following the war. He presciently and cogently argued that these debts would provide a breeding ground for German nationalism and militarism, commenting that the treaty was no more than a political grudge. His argument rested on the premise that under the agreement, Germany would be overburdened by war debt and consequently hindered from fully participating in the world economy. At the time, Germany was already one of the biggest economies in the world, and if it faltered, Keynes reasoned, so would the rest of Europe.[37]

Keynes's best-known work is *The General Theory of Employment, Interest, and Money*, which was written during the depths of the Depression and suggested possible causes and proposed solutions. Among other arguments, Keynes put forward the idea that the state needed to intervene in the economy during downturns. The timing of the publication of this book is significant. It was published in 1936 and by then many of Keynes's solutions had already been implemented. In the United States, for example, Franklin Delano Roosevelt's New Deal was first unveiled in 1933. But Roosevelt had neither the intellectual cachet nor sufficient evidence to justify this program. It was after the fact, then, that Keynes arrived on the scene to provide a well-reasoned and -argued justification for state intervention.

One did not need be an academic, or for that matter anticapitalist, to grasp that something had gone horribly wrong during the Depression. This was obvious to anyone who experienced it. The worldwide Depression did a respectable job of discrediting the capitalist system on its own, and in the eyes of ever-increasing numbers, particularly unemployed workers, socialism provided a viable alternative. But this alternative found few fans among the political elite in either Great Britain or North America. It is important to understand that at the time debates about capitalism and socialism were not just academic. Socialist political ideology, already popular around the world, had been put into practice with the Bolshevik Revolution of 1917. The question "Whither capitalism?" was one asked seriously at the time, and for that reason, particularly in North America, socialism was considered a serious threat by those in power.

The Great Depression, as it is often called, began in 1929 and would last for the bulk of the 1930s. Such an event was, in the words of Robert Heilbroner, "absurd, impossible, paradoxical, and inexplicable. But it was there."[38] It was as though the powers that be had wilfully exposed the chasm between theory and practice. All market economies were hit hard by this event, but nowhere did the Depression arrive with more force than in North America. In Canada, GDP fell from $6.4 billion in 1929 to $3.7 billion in 1934 and nearly one-quarter of the labour force was out of work. Not to be outdone, the United States was hit even worse. The economy shrank by 54 percent and construction fell by 90 percent. There was obvious wealth; at times it seemed there was too much. The problem was with its distribution, for the abundant wealth that did exist failed to reach those who most needed it. Crops were left unharvested and surplus food was dumped into the ocean. Warehouses throughout North America and the rest of the industrial world were overflowing. Everywhere there were gluts, but nobody was buying. Conventional economics, of course, was at odds to explain this contraction, both its severity and longevity. Most politicians, including then prime minister Richard Bedford Bennett of Canada, decided to simply wait out the downturn and allow the market to work things out. But such a moment failed to materialize, and political unrest and pressures from various interests eventually forced governments to act.

Keynes gave a much-needed intellectual legitimacy to the process. He wrote largely about the intricacies of investment, but his name is now mostly associated with deficit financing. His most lasting insight is that the Depression was caused by a lack of demand. As was the case with Smith, Keynes's focus became the consumer, but from an entirely different perspective. Whereas Smith addressed the welfare of the consumer, Keynes stressed the importance of the consumer's role in keeping the economy buoyant. Consumption, not thrift, Keynes argued, would breathe much-needed life back into the economy. The reason warehouses were filled to capacity was simple: People lacked the money to consume. Keynes rejected the conventional orthodoxy that wages would eventually fall to the point where workers would once again be hired, after which they would go on to consume. Lower wages meant less purchasing power, countered Keynes, and rather than solving the problem, they only exacerbated it. Fewer workers consuming directly translated into more bursting warehouses and idle factories. When millions of people were unemployed, as was the case in the Depression, this lack of aggregate demand ensured the economy would remain stagnant. This was in contrast to most economists, who argued that in the long run wages would increase, workers would take jobs, and prosperity would return. But Keynes said he was concerned about the short term for, as his famous reply goes, "In the long run we are all dead."[39]

Most governments did end up practising some form of Keynesianism, yet Western economies continued to be in a slump throughout the 1930s. It was not until the Second World War, when government intervention was practised in earnest, that the North American economy fully recovered. Following the war, most countries continued to implement Keynesian policies in various ways. In the 1950s and 1960s, unlike today, governments had plenty of financial resources to draw upon. Revenues no longer needed to sustain the voracious war effort were now available to fund other, primarily social, programs. In Canada, programs like Family Allowance were explicitly introduced with the intention of sustaining aggregate demand. The Keynesian welfare state had arrived.

Today's Relevance

How relevant are Keynes's ideas today? The middle way that Keynes introduced as a compromise between socialism and capitalism appears to be less meaningful today, as one of those poles, socialism, has turned into less of a threat. On a global basis, the counterbalance once provided by socialism has been greatly weakened by the collapse of the Soviet empire. Capitalism, in contrast, has not experienced a major crisis since the Depression, and consequently its critics are easy to ignore. While a considerable portion of the population continues to express concern about the excesses of capitalism, such analyses tend to fall on deaf ears, at least in the political arena. The champions of capitalism have garnered the kind of confidence that allows little room for alternatives.

Yet on the domestic front at least, Keynes continues to influence. To be fair, countries today practise a somewhat bastardized version of Keynesianism. Keynes encouraged governments to run deficits in times of economic decline, but warned they should retreat when the economy prospered. Despite this advice, governments today intervene through both busts and booms. As said, governments have found it much easier to drop the ideology of Keynesianism than its policies. For whatever reason—powerful interest groups and bureaucracies, fear of public backlash—governments continue to fund a vast array of programs. In Canada, for example, the various levels of government continue to pledge more funding for health care. The alacrity with which the Alberta government handed out $2.3 billion to compensate for higher utility bills illustrates that even fiscally conservative governments are eager to interfere in the market if they sense a political backlash on the radar screen. Central banks also very much toe the Keynesian line and regulate interest rates with an eye to economic growth, in contrast to the steady-hand approach of monetarism preached by conservatives. We will discuss more of Keynes's influence in the section on international institutions, but for now let it suffice to say that the mixed economy—part laissez-faire, part planned—is alive and well in the West.

Most important, Keynes's suggestions on the international front should be taken to heart. Keynes provides obvious credibility to state intervention on the national scale, which amounts to no less than a practical repudiation of free markets in the domestic sphere. Following this line of argument, it seems reasonable to question the wisdom of free markets in the international realm. Given the success of the German economy since the Second World War era—it is now the third-largest economy in the world—we must judge the billions of dollars that were poured into Germany under the auspices of the Marshall Plan to be a more successful tactic than the reparation payments the country was forced to endure following the First World War. There is a clear parallel here between the events in Germany following the First World War and contemporary Third World debts. Saddling Third World countries with enormous financial obligations, although not the consequence of war, is likely to produce similar outcomes. Forcing these countries to pay spiralling debt prevents them from having any real opportunity to join the world economy, and such conditions are as likely to breed militarism, discontent, and strife as when they were forced upon Germany in the interwar years.

Smith and Ricardo, and for that matter Keynes, wrote about events that were historically specific to their lifetimes. All wrote for posterity and assumed their theories were applicable to all places and times, or at least they have been interpreted that way. Smith railed against a corrupt state, Ricardo against greedy landowners, and Keynes against a quiescent state. Whereas Keynes's theory is still relevant today, things have changed considerably since Smith and Ricardo wrote. We no longer live in a world of manufactory where the labour supply is directly dependent on a worker's wage; neither do we live in a time when the majority of one's income goes to the purchasing of bread or when a tariff on grain might mean teetering over the edge into starvation. The state has been democratized since Smith's time and it no longer constitutes the monopoly playground of the elite. In short, both economically and socially, the economic world has evolved dramatically since the eighteenth and nineteenth centuries, and we need to be circumspect about making generalizations on the basis of observations made one hundred and fifty or two hundred years ago.

Canada was part of many of the events that we have just discussed: colonization, mercantilism, the first free trade era, and the Great Depression. In the next chapter, we are going to focus on how Canada's history fits into this background.

5

The one thing we learn from history is
that we do not learn from history.
—GEORG WILHELM HEGEL

THE HISTORY OF
FREE TRADE IN CANADA

THE HISTORY OF CANADA'S ECONOMY reveals two notable trends. First, Canada's exposure to the global economy has waxed and waned with no obvious ill effects on its own economy. It seems that Canadians have always been quick to adapt to changing economic conditions. Second, Canadians are, and always have been, divided about free trade. There has always been a sizable portion of the population that has supported free trade, countered by an equally large segment of the population that has opposed it. And so it is to this day. Not too much detail is needed to realize that this support, or lack of it, usually aligns with one's economic interests. Self-interest and power go a long way in understanding Canada's economic history. Not surprisingly, rather than adopting a position based on ideology, most industries choose to support whatever option appears to be most profitable at the time. Those destined to improve their standard of living from free trade are likely to support it; those who anticipate they will forfeit market share, become uncompetitive, or lose jobs are likely to oppose it. In this mix of interests, some people are better able to make their voices heard than others, and business is more influential and likely to get its way than, say, artists. This sometimes wide array of competing interests has resulted in a general lack of consensus on the topic of free trade, and there has never been a point in Canada's history when everyone has agreed on its desirability.

Explorer Interrupted

It is well known that the Americas, including what is now Canada, were settled long before they were colonized by Europeans. There is ample evidence that the Vikings had settled in what is now Newfoundland around the turn of the first millennium, but this proved to be little more than a visit. Permanent contact did not occur until the arrival of the Spanish, English, and French near the end of the fifteenth century. The encounter of European and indigenous cultures, which took centuries to encompass the whole continent, was not planned; neither peoples were even aware of the other's existence. Their eventual meeting was motivated by the very topic of this book, trade. During the fifteenth century, trade between Europe and Asia was already on the rise, and a number of adventurous and entrepreneurial Europeans, sponsored by an equally entrepreneurial monarchy, began searching for a water route to Asia. The reason for this was simple: Long distances were overly cumbersome to cover by land, and a water route would greatly facilitate the transportation of goods between Asia and Europe. In 1492, Christopher Columbus, a Genoese by birth and sponsored by the Spanish monarchy, was the first to search for such a route. But his destination, Asia, was interrupted by the rather large land mass of the Americas.[40] Only a few years later, in 1497, John Cabot, also originally from Genoa, but this time sponsored by Britain, sailed to North America and sighted the Newfoundland coast. Cabot was motivated by the same goal as Columbus, to find a trade route to Asia. By sailing farther north, Cabot hoped to circumvent the Americas and be presented with a clear passage to Asia. As we know now, he, too, failed to reach his final destination. But what he did find—fish—was of enough interest to keep the Europeans returning to that part of the world on a steady basis.

Although fishing off the coast of what is now Atlantic Canada has continued uninterrupted ever since, further exploration of that part of the continent was delayed for another thirty years. This time financed by France, and still partially motivated by the search for a new trade route to Asia, Jacques Cartier, beginning in 1534, undertook three expeditions during a period of just over a decade. On one of these trips, Cartier sailed up the St. Lawrence River and reached what is now Montreal. But just like Cabot before him, Cartier saw no reason to establish a permanent settlement.

The Fur Trade

For over a century after Cabot first sighted Eastern Canada, European fishers fished its fecund waters and then returned to their homes, never identifying a need to settle. At most, Europeans would go ashore to dry their fish and prepare them for transport. Even the fur trade at first took place on the margins: Europeans would meet Aboriginals on the coast of Newfoundland and later Gaspé to exchange furs for manufactured goods. A permanent European settlement was not established in what is now Canada until Samuel de Champlain founded Quebec in 1608, 111 years after Canada was first sighted by the Europeans. Before then, there had been no economic rationale to justify settlement—in most endeavours, New France was unable to compete with the British colonies to the south and with Europe itself. But with furs, the new colony finally had a product in which it could claim a competitive advantage. By that time, the fur industry had already undergone respectable growth. To wear fur, and above all beaver hats, had become the height of fashion in France, and while fur-bearing animals were indigenous to Northern Europe, demand greatly outstripped supply. This translated into a boom for the North American fur industry. The establishment of a permanent base, the French reasoned, would help them secure a monopoly over the fur trade. Again, mercantilism played an important role, and France founded the One Hundred Associates with the express objective of monopolizing trade in the new colony. But living conditions in New France were harsh and there was little to attract new immigrants. Consequently population growth was excruciatingly slow; only about twenty-five persons per annum. By 1645, close to four decades after it was founded, only six hundred Europeans called Quebec their home.

At this point, it is worth mentioning that the relationship between Europeans and Aboriginals was not always

antagonistic. In fact, for the first three centuries or so following contact, their relationship was symbiotic. The Europeans
required the co-operation of Aboriginals to supply them with
furs, and Aboriginals, in turn, found most useful the manufactured products they were able to acquire from the Europeans.
Some bands, such as the Ottawa and Algonquin, acted as
mediators between the Europeans and the more remote bands
that supplied the furs. These mediating bands quickly learned
the lessons of the free market and profited handsomely.
Gradually Europeans began taking a more active role in the
fur trade, first in transportation, and later in trapping as well.
Throughout this period, the Canadian economy slowly became
more diversified as the French, and later the British, established
agricultural settlements. The fur trade continued to play an
important role in the Canadian economy until 1870, at which
point it was eclipsed by industries such as agriculture, timber,
and shipbuilding. This transition, unfortunately, also spelled
the end of the co-operative relationship between Europeans
and Aboriginals. By the time of Confederation, resource
extraction and farming had become the leading economic
activities, and the assistance of Aboriginals was no longer
required. In fact, they were now considered to stand in the
way of economic progress.

The fur and the fishing industries, which dominated
Canadian international trade for the first couple of centuries,
set the tone for the Canadian economy to the present day. As
important, Canada's economy was utterly international right
from its very beginnings. In those early days nearly all products, whether fish or fur, found their way back to Europe.
Furthermore, the survival of Canada's settlers, as well as that
of the Aboriginals who participated in the fur trade, depended

on these international markets. Had it not been for those foreign markets, European immigrants would likely have bypassed Canada. Its harsh climate and inhospitable landscape did not make it an easy place to make a living. But its natural resources meant there were plenty of economic opportunities for exports. Canada's protracted settlement, which took place over a period of centuries, was motivated by the desire to control, manage, and profit from this trade.

Mercantilism

The fundamental nature of Canada's economy has remained the same throughout its entire history. It always has been, and continues to be, a supplier of raw resources, usually referred to as staples, first to Europe and then the United States. In the early mercantilist days, it was fish, timber, wheat, and selected natural resources. Today it continues to be lumber and minerals, in addition to electricity and oil. In other words, the character of the Canadian economy has not changed in any significant way since contact over five hundred years ago.[41] The age of mercantilism contributes an important chapter to this history. This era overlaps with the fur trade at one end and a diversified and mature economy at the other. At its heart, the doctrine of mercantilism, practised by various European empires from the sixteenth century until the mid-nineteenth century, entailed importing resources from the colonies while supplying them with manufactured products. The success of this type of economy depended on tariff protection and monopolized markets. Based on these policies, mercantilism turned out to provide a much-needed boost to the Canadian economy. For Canada, this period began

in the late seventeenth century when the French minister of
the marine, Jean Baptiste Colbert, undertook to exploit the
colony of New France for the benefit of the mother country.
According to the elemental doctrines of mercantilism,
Canada's role was to provide staples such as furs and timber.
The destination of these staples included not only France, but
also its other colonies, such as the West Indies. France in turn,
would supply its colonies with manufactured products. From a
market perspective, these preferential arrangements did not
make a whole lot of economic sense. New England was closer
to the French West Indies than New France, and furthermore,
the English colonies were blessed with a more benign climate
for food production. But this did not matter to France, and
based on the tenets of mercantilism, it gave preference to its
own, albeit more distant and less competitive, territories.

After the French ceded Quebec to the British in 1759,
Britain enforced its own mercantilist policies. Again, this was
to the great advantage of the Canadian provinces, which
were decidedly uncompetitive in comparison with the soon-
independent American states (1776). Canada's ample territories could be used to grow wheat, but the same was true for the
United States, which had a longer growing season. In addition
to a better climate, New England had a much larger population, and was thus able to lay claim to a more diversified
market. It also made little economic sense for Great Britain to
bring timber all the way from Canada, when instead it could
import it from the much closer Baltic states. In other words,
the market did not look favourably upon Canada. By all
accounts, it was a failure and destined to remain wilderness.

But, of course, the market did not prevail and mercantilism
did. This arrangement was particularly beneficial for Canada

in its early history. Most important to Canada's development were preferential duties and the Navigation Acts. Higher tariffs on products originating outside of the British Empire meant Canada was able to compete with the United States and other European countries. As the Canadian economy matured, it began specializing in such activities as shipbuilding, which was of immense benefit to the Maritimes and Lower Canada (Quebec) in the first half of the nineteenth century. As already discussed, the Navigation Acts decreed that goods hailing from within the empire had to be transported on British-built and British-owned ships. This translated into a boom for Canadian shipbuilders that might not otherwise have occurred. The export of Canadian staples was further aided by the Embargo Act of 1807, which prohibited American states from trading with Europe, and the Non-Intercourse Act of 1809, which re-established trade with Europe with the exclusion of France and England, the latter being Canada's most important market.

It should be apparent by now that the protectionist policies of the mercantilist era were of invaluable benefit to the Canadian colonies. Had free trade prevailed, Canada's resources would have remained unexploited, and it is anyone's guess how its history would have differed. Most crucial to Canada's economic development was that when Great Britain finally did introduce free trade in the mid-nineteenth century, Canada had matured to the point that it was able to survive on its own. By then, the Canadian economy had established a firm foothold in many important industries, including timber, shipbuilding, and wheat. Meanwhile, as Canada's population grew, its economy became more diversified. A larger population undergirded a healthy domestic market that led to increased specialization. Had free trade been adopted instead of mercantilism, Canada's economy would no doubt have eventually matured, but this progress would have been delayed by a considerable margin of time and surely determined a different political history. In short, mercantilism amounted to a *quid pro quo*, in which both sides benefited considerably. Without the advantages afforded by mercantilism, colonization would have been unprofitable for France and Britain; as well, Canada would have remained uncompetitive in most industries. In the absence of preferential treatment, Canada would likely have been slowly taken over by its neighbour to the south. America slowly grew westward, and if it had not been for the presence of the French and the British, there is no reason to believe that it would not have expanded northward, too. In other words, without mercantilism Canada as a separate political entity would likely not exist today.

The First Free Trade Era

This is not to argue that Canada should reinstate mercantilism. As we saw in chapter 2, mercantilism was the breeding ground for a great deal of corruption and in this capacity served as an easy mark for Smith's *The Wealth*. Ricardo's target, the Corn Laws, was also associated with mercantilism. Given these well-reasoned attacks, and the derision mercantilism invariably meets today, there may be little good that can be said of it. Moreover, when mercantilism was dismantled in the middle of the nineteenth century, the move had widespread public support. But, as said, mercantilism provided Canada with a much-needed economic foundation. For this reason, Canada was less than enthusiastic about the end of mercantilism and the introduction of free trade. With preferential treatment gone, many industries feared for their very survival. As frequently happens as a result of rapid change, the cessation of imperial preference initially produced some panic. The business community, specifically the English-speaking business elites in Montreal and Quebec, proposed the radical solution of joining the United States. The Annexation Association, as it called itself, was founded in 1849 and lasted until 1854, when the Reciprocity Treaty with the United States sabotaged its raison d'être. But the end of mercantilism did not spell disaster for Canadian markets. Sales of wheat and lumber to Britain actually continued to increase, despite a reduction in preferential tariffs, or sometimes their outright elimination. Furthermore, as the population increased in Canada, farmers switched to other, more profitable products, such as fruits and vegetables, dairy products and meats.[42]

Reciprocity Treaty of 1854

With the end of mercantilism and British Imperial preference, Canada, an economy founded on international trade, lost its most important trading partner. This situation was further exacerbated by the increasingly protectionist tendencies of the United States. In order to stem the protectionist tide, Canada felt, just as it would over 130 years later, that its interests would be best served by a free trade agreement. After five years of negotiations with a much less enthusiastic United States, Canada (which included the Province of Canada as well as the eastern provinces) signed its first Reciprocity Treaty with the United States in 1854. This deal was a far cry from the comprehensive trade deals of today and covered only natural resources. Yet Canada felt it needed a deal badly, and it was willing to give up much to get it. Or at least exporters of raw materials wanted it badly, and they were willing to sell out other industries. Canada eventually ended up offering the United States access to the St. Lawrence Seaway as well as to the fecund fishing grounds off the east coast, provisions that were vociferously opposed by some of the eastern provinces. Despite considerable resistance, a deal was struck. But it would last only a dozen years. In 1866, the United States unilaterally abrogated the treaty because of Canada's support of the North in the Civil War. Once again Canada was left without a favoured trading partner. It lost preferential access to Great Britain because it embraced free trade and was kept out of the American market because it rejected the very same thing.

Only a year later, in 1867, the United Province of Canada (Quebec and Ontario) and Nova Scotia and New Brunswick joined in a political union to create the Dominion of Canada. This was partially motivated by the desire to at least guarantee free trade among the British North American provinces, and in this sense one could argue that Canada itself was a product of free trade.[43] Yet this union far from satisfied Canada's appetite for foreign markets. Canada had an almost unlimited store of resources, of which it could consume only a minuscule portion, and in order to prosper it needed to export its surpluses. And the United States, with more than ten times the population of Canada, was the logical solution to Canada's export woes. Geographical proximity meant that even in the absence of a formal trading arrangement, the United States became an increasingly important trading partner to Canada. And the more important the American market became, the more nervous Canada became about losing it. A rise in protectionism would surely have had grave consequences for Canada, and to avert this possibility, it doggedly hounded the United States to sign some kind of agreement. Most of the proposed deals included free trade in resources only, which is really all Canada needed anyway, although manufactured products were sometimes put on the table. The desire to clinch a deal meant that negotiations between Canada and the United States were ongoing, but all efforts proved fruitless. After the demise of the first Reciprocity Treaty in 1866, three further attempts to secure a deal, in 1869, 1871, and 1874, all resulted in failure.

After this string of overtures was rejected by the American administration, Canada retaliated with its own protectionist policies. In 1879, the Conservative Party, under the leadership of John A. Macdonald, introduced the National Policy, which raised tariffs on manufactured goods coming into Canada. One of the objectives of this policy was to establish a Canadian manufacturing base; another was to change the direction of trade from north-south to east-west. The National Policy would, under various guises, last for well over a century, and did not come to an official end until 1989, when it was replaced by the Canada US Free Trade Agreement (FTA).

In the current political and economic climate, calls for government intervention are all too easy to dismiss, but Canada's history illustrates that the state's role need not be detrimental. The nationalistic policies practised by the Canadian government around the turn of the twentieth century were widely supported and played an important role in keeping the country together. Following Confederation, nation building was very much on the government's mind, and the National Policy was one of the most important policy initiatives that contributed towards this end. By encouraging east-west trade, the policy strengthened ties between Canada's vast and underdeveloped regions. The construction of canals and, more important, the later building of a national railroad further encouraged domestic trade. In this, government played a central role, often with the full support of business, which profited handsomely from these endeavours. There are various opinions on how this policy affected Canada, but most historians agree that it at least helped establish nascent industries. It also prompted American corporations to locate branch plants in Canada, which had positive consequences in terms of technology transfers and employment.

Now let us take a closer look at what kind of effect the National Policy had on the economy. For the first part of the 1870s, the Canadian economy stagnated, as did the rest of the world economy. When the recession ended towards the middle of that decade, the Canadian economy picked up substantially. The National Policy was introduced in 1879, and without any noticeable effects on the economy. The economy continued to stagnate throughout the 1880s up until the mid-1890s. From then on, fortunes changed and the Canadian economy grew rapidly until the beginning of the First World War. During this growth spurt Canada even managed to outperform the American economy. But this prosperity probably had less to do with Canada's protectionist trade policies than with the general health of the global economy. The period between 1870 and 1913 was the most prosperous period the world economy had undergone up to that point, and all industrial economies, including those of

Canada and the United States, did well by it.[44] World trade also increased substantially during this period. At the time, most of Canada's trade was with Great Britain, although there was a considerable increase in imports from the United States. All this occurred despite the absence of a formal trade agreement, as both Canada and the United States had policies in place that were blatantly protectionist and nationalistic.

This is not to say that free trade was a dead issue. Although it continued to be official government policy, there was ongoing opposition to the National Policy, and Canada continued in its efforts to secure a trading agreement with at least one of its two largest trading partners. It attempted to re-establish some sort of preferential arrangement with Great Britain as well as to negotiate a free trade deal with the United States. The latter found considerable support among selected sectors of the Canadian economy, which continued to exert pressure on the government to secure a deal. As one would expect, free trade was supported by those who depended on foreign markets to sell their surplus, such as farmers and people in other resource industries. Again for reasons of self-interest, those who had to compete with manufacturing industries in the United States opposed a free trade deal. Wilfrid Laurier's Liberals, first elected in 1896, were sympathetic to the persistent demands for free trade, and it was not for lack of trying that they failed to strike a deal. During their fifteen years in government, the Liberals approached the United States several times with the intent of negotiating an agreement. But just like in the 1860s and 1870s, Canada was faced with a reluctant partner. It was not so much that the United States outright dismissed free trade; it wanted more than Canada was willing to offer. Rather than mere reciprocity, the United States sought a commercial union, which Canada rejected outright for fear that it would lead down the inevitable road of annexation.

To summarize, over a period that spanned more than four decades, Canada and the United States flirted with the issue of free trade. But the United States, at least for the most part, did not even want to dance. Sure, it would think about it if a more permanent union were in the future, but Canada was, frankly speaking, just not ready for that kind of commitment. Given this divergence in objectives, an agreement was never reached. All this nothingness flared into a national event with the federal election of 1911. This time it was the Americans who approached Canada. The United States was even willing to downgrade its usual demands for a much less desirable, at least in the eyes of Canadians, commercial union. Given Canada's ongoing efforts to secure access to the American market, it is no surprise that the United States found a willing partner in Canada. All the terms of the treaty were agreed upon and it looked like a done deal when a groundswell of opposition emerged and Laurier was forced to call an election. In direct contrast to the 1988 election, the Liberals ran on a platform of reciprocity, whereas the Conservatives under Robert Borden advocated continuation of the National Policy (still in place despite fifteen years of Liberal rule). Borden was not above using fear tactics, and warned of the inevitability of annexation once a deal was signed, which undoubtedly swayed many Canadians to vote against reciprocity. In the end, Borden's win was decisive, thanks primarily to the backing of powerful manufacturing interests in Ontario. Borden won seventy-three out of eighty-six seats, a resounding repudiation of free trade, it seems. But this opposition was not as overwhelming as the distribution of seats would make it appear. According to another indicator, the popular vote, Borden received 51 percent of the vote, a bare majority. Laurier received a respectable 48 percent (1 percent of the vote went to other parties). This election showed that free trade, despite all appearances of being a relative non-issue for over forty years, was a topic that divided the country.

Over the next thirty-five years the world experienced three cataclysmic events that combined to overshadow economic issues like free trade: two world wars separated by a depression. Three years after the 1911 election, the First World War broke out and Canada immediately came to the aid of its ally Great Britain. The war turned out to be a boon for Canadian exports, but the instability of the post-war years erased any gains made during the conflict. The world economy went through a brief growth spurt in the 1920s, which fizzled as quickly as it came and gave way to the Depression of the 1930s. In reaction to the economic collapse, the United States became even more insular and raised tariffs on all imports, including those from Canada. Thus over a century and a half of protectionism culminated in the Smoot Hawley Tariff of 1930. This policy convinced Prime Minister Bennett that Canada needed to re-establish ties with its old friend, Great Britain, and in 1932, Canada and several other countries signed a series of bilateral trade deals known as the Ottawa Agreements. But these deals failed to give the Canadian economy the boost it needed and once again proposals surfaced for a trade agreement with the United States. And yet again, the Americans remained cool to the idea. But this evasiveness would not last long. When Roosevelt came to power in 1933, Canada was presented with the first trade-friendly administration in many years. In 1935, only five years after it was first introduced, the Smoot Hawley Tariff was dismantled by the United States. This marked the first change in direction in America's trade policy since the demise of the Reciprocity Treaty of 1854, and the first time the country had become actively involved in opening its borders since American independence. Finally, after a century and a half of almost uninterrupted protectionism, the United States embraced free trade, a policy direction it has, at least officially, not veered from since.

Torn between Two Lovers

The most momentous events of the twentieth century, the two world wars and the Depression, all occurred before the century even reached the halfway mark. The tumult of that era overshadowed the power struggle for supremacy between two world powers, Great Britain and the United States. This transition came to play a decisive role in Canada's economic history. It was during the period spanning the two world wars that Canada shifted its allegiance from its past mentor, Great Britain, to that of the newly emerging world power, the United States. This gradual transformation is reflected in trade statistics. Since Confederation, Canada's trade has primarily been with Europe (and most of that with Great Britain) and the United States. In general terms, Britain was the preferred trading partner in the nineteenth century. During the first half of the twentieth century, Canada traded roughly equally between the old empire, Great Britain, and the new, the United States. This period was marked by political and economic unrest on a global basis and it seems that Canada was either hesitant or unable to get a firm commitment from either power. Throughout this period Canada vacillated between re-establishing ties with Great Britain and establishing new ones with the United States.

It was not until the second half of the twentieth century that there was a decisive end to this uncertainty. After the Second World War, Canada's trade and economic dependence shifted squarely to the United States. This is despite several attempts to nationalize the Canadian economy with such National Policy–like initiatives as the National Energy Policy (NEP) and the Foreign Investment Review Agency (FIRA). The GATT (General Agreement on Tariffs and Trade) negotiations resulted in tariffs being lowered around the world, meaning that Canada's position vis-à-vis the rest of the world was equally favourable to that of the United States. But rather than becoming more globalized (that is, trading with countries other than the United States), Canada's trade became markedly more continentalized. In 1945, exports as a percentage of GDP to the United States hovered around 7 percent, about the same amount destined for Europe. By 1980, exports to the United States more than doubled to 15 percent, while exports to Europe decreased to around 3 percent. In the mid-1980s, when free trade was first discussed after a long absence, exports to the United States had shot up to 20 percent of GDP; meanwhile, exports to Europe dropped even further—to about 2.5 percent of GDP. The Canadian economy was becoming increasingly continentalized and all this without any formal trade agreement. In comparison, other regions of the world failed to play a significant role in Canada's trade. To this day, exports to Asia amount to less than 3 percent of Canada's GDP (as do imports), and Africa, South America, and Australia are virtually shut out of the Canadian economy, with combined exports amounting to less than 2 percent of Canada's GDP.

The ever-increasing importance of American markets to the Canadian economy should be obvious by this point. This development occurred gradually but unabated from the Second World War onwards and was already well in place before the introduction of the Canada US Free Trade Agreement in 1989. From that perspective, one can understand the indifference that some politicians exhibited towards negotiations when they first began in 1986. This agreement would amount to little more than official recognition of a trend that had been unfolding for the past three decades—the deal could well be interpreted as no more than a formality. At best, it would guarantee access to the lucrative American market, something for which many Canadian industries have been clamouring for decades. At worst, it would entrench the status quo.

But the continental trade deal proved to be no mere formality. At first, opposition to the deal appeared muted. The New Democratic Party (NDP), aware of the voluminous trade between the two countries, saw little need to provide leadership on the issue. But slowly a groundswell of resistance mounted. Opposition, just as in the election of 1911, appeared to come out of nowhere, catching many politicians off guard. But the ensuing debate was fought along familiar lines, and echoed century-old fears. Leading up to the 1988 election, anxiety about annexation resurfaced, and questions of national and cultural sovereignty were vigorously debated. And again just like in 1911, the party in government, the

Progressive Conservatives, was forced to call an election. On the left, it was the Action Canada Network, an umbrella group of interests that included labour and a series of non-governmental organizations, that first fought free trade. The campaign leading up to the election was at times emotionally charged and neither side was above using fear tactics. Historically strong proponents of free trade, the Liberals were compelled to switch sides and fight against it. The Liberals, siding with the left, warned of the political dangers inherent in a free trade agreement with the United States. In probably the most memorable quote of the campaign, and certainly his political career, Liberal leader John Turner warned that national sovereignty was at stake. "Any country that is willing to surrender economic levers inevitably yields levers politically and surrenders a large chunk of its ability to remain a sovereign nation. I don't believe our future depends on our yielding those economic levers of sovereignty to become a junior partner in Fortress North America to the United States."[45] In contrast, the Progressive Conservatives, backed by a powerful business lobby, warned that if Canadians did not embrace free trade, Canada would suffer and be left behind in the new global economy. The left saw doom and gloom if free trade became a reality; the right predicted the same if the deal was defeated. Neither option was probably all that appealing to Canadians.

As we saw, the popular vote in the 1911 election was split right down the middle. In 1988, the country was equally divided, although results were a little more lopsided. The Progressive Conservatives were able to garner only 43 percent of the popular vote, which approximately reflected Canadian public opinion on free trade. In terms of seats, however,

Canadians were faced with a completely different outcome and they watched as Mulroney was handed another clear majority: The Progressive Conservatives were able to win 169 of the 295 available seats. The Liberals, running on an anti–free trade platform, were able to win only 83 seats, with the NDP taking the remaining 43 seats.

One really has to wonder how sincere the Liberals were when they campaigned against free trade, and one suspects its position was more based on political opportunism than heart-felt conviction. Their subsequent behaviour certainly points in that direction. After another five years in government, the Progressive Conservatives lost the 1993 election in what can only be described as spectacular fashion and managed to hold on to just two seats. The Liberals once again ran on an anti–free trade platform, although by then the topic had lost considerable force. By the time the 1993 election rolled around, the Canada US Free Trade Agreement was slated to be upgraded to the North American Free Trade Agreement (NAFTA), which was essentially the Canada US Free Trade Agreement plus Mexico. As part of their election campaign, the Liberals promised to scuttle the deal. The Liberals did win the election, with a comfortable majority, one might add, but conveniently forgot about that particular promise, and NAFTA is still very much in place today. In fact, ever since they were first re-elected in 1993, the Liberals have proven to be at least as keen on free trade as the Progressive Conservatives were during their reign. It seems the Liberals are willing to support anything as long as it has the word "free" or "trade" in it, including the World Trade Organization, Asia Pacific Economic Cooperation (APEC), and the Free Trade Agreement of the Americas (FTAA). This forces one to conclude that the anti–free trade stance the party adopted between 1988 and 1993 had more to do with fulfilling its role as "Her Majesty's Royal Opposition" than with any genuine concern about the consequences of free trade. The king is dead; long live the king.

The free trade agreements (FTA and NAFTA) only served to buttress the close economic ties that Canada had established with the United States over the previous forty years. Exports to the United States went as high as 25 percent of GDP and currently comprise close to 70 percent of Canada's total exports. So at least in terms of increasing trade with the United States, the agreements have been a success. But as we learned in previous chapters, the amount of trade is not necessarily a good indicator of the success of a trade agreement. Rather, we want to know about economic growth, which in this instance has not met with the same success. What is of note is how in both free trade elections political outcomes meshed with the objectives of corporate interests. In 1911, business opposed a deal, and in 1988 it supported it; both times, business was able to get what it wanted.

Conclusion

Looking back on Canada's history it is difficult to draw any definitive conclusions about the consequences, whether good or bad, of free trade. In its early days, Canada's economy depended on the preferential treatment extended under the mercantilist system by France and then Britain. Throughout this era of tightly orchestrated trade, Canada's economy grew slowly; but at least it grew, which might not have been the case otherwise. This era came to a sudden end in the mid-1840s, when Great Britain introduced free trade. Initially, Canadian farmers and businesses were panicked about losing favoured access to British markets, but they quickly adapted and diversified. Canadians also did well under its first Reciprocity Treaty with the United States in the 1850s and 1860s. The economy even continued to grow when the United States unilaterally abrogated that deal in 1866. After repeated attempts, all in vain, Canada was left without a trade deal with the Americans and embarked on a policy of protectionism of its own. For over a century, the National Policy dominated, and throughout, the Canadian economy did not falter, except for a brief spell during the Depression. The economy performed especially well after the Second World War, but that growth slowed in the mid-1970s. Many economists and politicians have argued that the slowdown was caused by too much government interference, and offered free trade, among other things, as a solution. In 1989, after waiting for well over a century, free traders finally witnessed the signing of another deal with the United States. Almost a decade and a half later, the Canadian economy is still humming along. How long free trade will reign supreme is anyone's guess, but history suggests it will not be forever. History also suggests that whatever the policy, its impact on the economy will be less than spectacular.

It is difficult to speculate how Canada's economy would have performed differently had free trade prevailed instead of the National Policy between the years of 1879 and 1989. Canada pursued free trade, as we saw, with varying degrees of enthusiasm throughout this period. The decision to have free trade was, of course, not Canada's alone to make, and it needed the consent of at least one other partner. The most coveted of these candidates, the United States, showed itself to be interminably reluctant. Yet even if it had acquiesced, it seems unlikely that Canada's economy would have performed that much differently. Keeping in mind the thesis of this book, the effect of more or less trade would have been insignificant compared with that of other developments, such as worldwide depressions, technological advancements, wars, and population growth. Seen from another angle, Canada's economy enjoyed robust growth, with only few exceptions, throughout the 110 years that the National Policy prevailed, and there is no reason to believe it would have performed that much better, or for that matter worse, had free trade been the dominant economic policy. Things, however, would likely have been different had free trade dominated in Canada's early history. From contact in the late fifteenth century to the mid-1800s, Canada depended on the protected markets provided by the French and British empires. Without the benefits of subsidies and preferential access, as well as military aid from France and Great Britain, it is doubtful that Canada would have survived to become its own country.

6

Those in power only want to perpetuate it.
—JUSTICE WILLIAM O. DOUGLAS

Nobody talks more of free enterprise and competition and
of the best man winning than the man who inherited his
father's store or farm.
—C. WRIGHT MILLS

WORLD TRADE:
THE GATT AND THE WTO

We HAVE GONE INTO SOME DETAIL about how free trade works in
theory. Now it is time to examine how these issues unfold in
the practical realm. Free trade appears to have widespread
support, but at the same time, it seems difficult to enforce. In
this chapter we are going to look at some of the conflicting
interests, both national and international, that have thwarted
a smooth-functioning global system of trade, and will likely
continue to do so in the foreseeable future.

Immediately following the Second World War, a number of
institutions were established to regulate the world economy,

the World Bank and the IMF being the most prominent among them. However, it would be a different story for free trade, as the WTO would not be established for another fifty years. The reason for this delay can essentially be attributed to a lack of consensus among negotiating countries. For many reasons, some of which will be elaborated on below, an agreement proved to be unworkable. Yet the need for an institution to oversee international trade endured. Negotiations towards this end were ongoing, but it took close to a half century before enough consensus existed for this institution to be established. This did not occur until 1995. But just because there is now an institution does not automatically mean that these differences have been resolved. This chapter will trace the beginnings of the ITO (International Trade Organization), thereby highlighting the clash of interests that makes free trade such an impossible goal. This will be followed by a section on the GATT and its principles. The conclusion will list some reasons why free trade is not likely to be achieved, and therefore, the WTO need not be feared.

History of the GATT and the WTO

The public image cultivated by the WTO, as well as the bulk of news reporting on the topic of free trade, generally involves putting on a brave face. Observations about the inevitability of free trade, both for and against, further contribute to the apparent consensus that free trade is a reality. Scaremongering—for example, talk about the loss of sovereignty, or the benefits lost if we close our borders—reinforces the monolithic consensus, whether good or bad, that is free trade. Yet such a consensus does not exist. Huge divisions endure not only between those who support and oppose free trade, but also within those two camps. These divisions—multiple, far-reaching, and possibly irreconcilable—are not new and have plagued free trade negotiations from their very beginnings. Multinational corporations are not going to rule the world, as they have conflicting interests, as well as interests that clash with those of the state. This alone should put at ease those readers who are concerned about Cassandra-like predictions of free trade.

The history of the GATT is by no means a straightforward one and is marked by few successes and many setbacks. In some ways, given all the different agendas that are normally brought to the table, it is almost a miracle that countries are still negotiating at all. Key to understanding the negotiating process is recognizing that not all countries, or interest groups within these countries, are equally powerful. Europe is more powerful than Canada, and business more so than environmental groups. And it is a very powerful United States, often spurred on by powerful export interests, that is most influential when it comes to the negotiation of trade agreements such as the GATT. It is no exaggeration to say that the WTO would not exist in its present form were it not for the United States. In light of that country's political and economic dominance, less powerful interests, such as labour, and smaller countries, such as Chile or Sweden—to say nothing of Bahrain or Cuba—have little say in the future direction of the WTO.

Groundwork: The Depression
Many accounts see the opening of markets following the Second World War as an altruistic act forced upon the world by the United States in order to safeguard a stable post-war

economy. This version portrays the United States as hero, a society that relegated national to international interests. By rejecting protectionism, the United States magnanimously ignored its own welfare, or at least this is the version it would like the rest of the world to believe. Another interpretation, one that is put forward here, is that free trade was a practical decision based on business and political interests that happened to align. In other words, the decision to open markets was not an ideological but a pragmatic one.

If it was not all that apparent in the first half of the twentieth century that Great Britain was no longer the world's dominant power, the United States was going to do everything in its power to crush any doubt about this in the second. The Second World War was a turning point in this development, as it impoverished Great Britain and enriched the United States. Upon the close of the Second World War, the United States was, to borrow a sports metaphor, the undisputed heavyweight champion of the world. With most of Europe and Japan in ruins, the United States accounted for almost two-thirds of the world's manufacturing output and one-third of the gross world product (the sum of the gross domestic product of all countries). American foreign policy, including the IMF and the World Bank, as well as the GATT, was going to be critical in furthering this American dominance. In this context, free trade can be seen as just another component of a well-orchestrated policy mix. The introduction of free trade was in stark contrast to over a century and a half of protectionism, which culminated in the Smoot Hawley Tariff in 1930. While there was scattered opposition to free trade in the United States following the Second World War, this opposition paled in comparison with the wide support free trade received from both industry and labour. With Europe and Japan virtually destroyed, American industries had little to lose and everything to gain. Big business—and primarily export-oriented corporations, such as GE, IBM, and Standard Oil—was solidly behind the opening of markets. For capital, it meant increased profits, for labour, an abundance of jobs.

The gradual embracing of free trade by the United States diverged somewhat from the attitude of Great Britain. Since the repeal of the Corn Laws in 1846, Great Britain had, again with few exceptions, been an unwavering proponent of free trade. Following the Depression, however, Great Britain reverted to a moderate version of protectionism, feeling its interests would be best served by refocusing its energies on its old empire. In 1934, the members of the newly formed British Commonwealth signed a series of bilateral agreements, known as the Ottawa Agreements.[46] But the United States wanted nothing to do with these agreements because it feared they could block its access to some potentially lucrative markets. From that perspective, free trade was going to be decisive in the battle over who would dominate the post-war economy.

The ITO (International Trade Organization)

Discussions about free trade first began with the Atlantic Charter of 1941, an agreement that eventually provided the basis for the UN Charter. The Atlantic Charter was hammered out by the United States and Great Britain on a ship off the coast of Newfoundland. The following year, in 1942, twenty-six countries signed the charter. In addition to accepting provisions about democratic rule and the location of international borders, participating countries agreed to co-operate economically and trade freely amongst each other. In 1944, in Bretton Woods, New Hampshire, further negotiations resulted in the subsequent founding of the IMF and the World Bank. The fact that trade negotiations did not result in a similar institution illustrates how competing national interests made consensus difficult.

The ITO was slated to be the outcome of the negotiations that took place throughout and shortly after the war. When the UN was officially founded in 1945 in San Francisco, it ratified the IMF and World Bank but not the ITO. Nevertheless, talks continued. On October 30, 1947, twenty-three countries convened in Cuba to negotiate tariff reductions, the document in process already being called the GATT. These meetings were officially known as the UN Conference on Trade and Employment, hinting that in the GATT's formative stages, the focus was not exclusively on trade but also labour. Canada was an enthusiastic participant in these negotiations for several reasons. In the past, Canada had often enjoyed preferential access to either the United States or Great Britain; sometimes neither, but never both at once. Canada realized that with a multilateral agreement it could for the first time have access to both markets. This made the GATT "a potent vehicle for promoting Canadian trade objectives."[47]

The first draft of the ITO charter was essentially written by the United States and naturally reflected both its interests and strengths. Open markets in other countries would no doubt benefit its powerful export industries. On the other hand, the United States conveniently ignored some of its own questionable trade practices. Australia sought to include a provision that would allow countries to protect struggling new industries, but the United States vehemently opposed any protectionist measures that could potentially block access to its industries. Yet the United States saw nothing wrong in subsidizing its agricultural industries, which other countries naturally disapproved of. Canada, in turn, wanted it all: It wanted to continue to take advantage of its so-called imperial preferences as well as to have free trade with the United States. There were also divisions within the United States, specifically between the administration and business. American multinationals lobbied for strict foreign invest-ment rules, similar to those of the contemporary Multilateral Agreement on Investment (MAI) and Agreement on Trade-Related Investment Measures (TRIMS), but the US govern-ment feared these would be given short shrift by other countries, on the grounds that these rules would encroach on their sovereignty.

The biggest rift, however, proved to be a difference of opinion between the United States and Great Britain over a more liberalized version of the pact and one that allowed a modicum of state intervention. While Canada shared a free market ideology with the United States, Great Britain, France, and Australia, as well as the majority of Third World countries, supported a more state-centred version. The latter position was informed by Keynes, and included provisions about full employment, employment standards, and assistance to poor countries. This tug of war between opposing objec-tives—between full employment policies and free trade only, between laissez-faire and intervention—was never properly resolved and eventually paved the way for the death of the deal. And while the Keynesian version officially fell by the wayside with the demise of the ITO, it continues to haunt debates on free trade to this day.

For all the reasons just listed, support for the ITO was generally weak around the world. Familiar worries about sovereignty were raised, with both the First and Third world countries expressing concern about the power the United States would wield within the organization.[48] Early on, the United States proposed that the ITO votes be based on economic power, an idea that, for obvious reasons, was particularly unpalatable to poor countries. This idea resurfaces periodically to this day, but understandably, gets little support. Great Britain was also concerned about how a worldwide agreement would compromise its ability to enforce its empire preferences under the Ottawa Agreements, which suited its present purposes fine.

But none of these concerns ever amounted to anything, as the Truman administration withdrew the deal before passing it on to Congress. Opposition in the United States coalesced around the labour clause. But even countries that supported the agreement were reluctant to sign. While it is fashionable to blame the United States for scuttling the deal, it received support from virtually no one. Many countries, believing that the ITO would work only if the United States ratified the agreement, waited for it to take the lead. But they did so in vain. The original charter had been so diluted by the input of a multitude of countries that the United States no longer believed the charter reflected its interests. Other countries also had their reasons. Europe was mired in economic problems, with the Marshall Plan stealing the political and economic spotlight. In the end, the provisional charter, which was signed by fifty-three out of fifty-six delegates, failed to be ratified by nearly all governments. Argentina and Poland rejected it outright; Turkey promised to sign later. The rest of the delegates took it back to their respective countries, where the deal died fifty-two different deaths. The only country to actually ratify the agreement was Liberia. This left the GATT as a mere agreement, and not the institution it was originally intended to be. With the death of the ITO, the United States came out the big winner, as labour issues were finally abandoned. By jettisoning all other responsibilities, the talks were finally free to focus on trade.

What can we learn from these talks? One, the vestiges of mercantilism prevailed (exports good, imports bad). No country, no matter how much it professed to support free trade, was immune to this mercantilist logic and this perspective continues to colour the attitudes of participating countries to this day. Based on this rational approach to economics, we find that countries champion free trade when they are in a competitive position and advocate protectionism when they are not. Calls for protectionism are loudest when an industry is weak, which usually happens at its dawn (the automobile industry in Australia after the war) or its eve (agriculture in Europe).

The talks that preceded the death of the ITO are of note because they set the tone for all subsequent trade negotiations. The issue of agriculture continues to hamper consensus and constitutes the core of the tension between the First and Third worlds. Less powerful economies are concerned about American dominance, and issues of sovereignty surface on an ongoing basis. For this and many other reasons, the road to the WTO in 1995 was a rocky one. The flouting of rules, particularly by the United States, made a deal increasingly less likely. Near the end of the 1980s and into the early 1990s, it looked as though the GATT was heading towards extinction.

In 1991, the well-known economist Lester Thurow declared that the GATT was dead and postulated that free trade was going to be replaced by a new era of protectionism. But Thurow's prognostications proved to be mistaken and, again because of powerful US export interests, there was a resurgence of interest in the GATT. This time, these interests were no longer manufacturing industries, like steel and automobiles, but rather knowledge industries, like pharmaceuticals, telecommunications, financial services, and biotechnology.

The GATT Now

The terms *GATT* and *WTO* are often used interchangeably, which in itself does not constitute a problem, as both are about free trade. In the interest of precision, however, it should be noted that the GATT is only one of several, albeit the initial and best-known, trade agreements under the auspices of the WTO. In short, the GATT is the document and the WTO the institution that enforces that agreement. The GATT, in this sense, is similar to any other agreement or charter, say the Canadian Charter, that constitutes a set of rules, and the WTO is the court that enforces those rules. Much of this confusion arises from the fact that for nearly five decades, from 1947 to 1995, there was no institution that acted as head of world trade (the ITO was initially planned as such). Consequently the abbreviation *GATT* came to stand for both the document and the institution. Once the WTO came on the scene in 1995, people continued to use *GATT* for both, either because they did not know or did not care; the GATT, however, is just an agreement.

Of the twenty-eight agreements regulated by the WTO, the GATT is by far the best known. The current agreement is sometimes identified by its year, as in the GATT 1994, so as to distinguish it from the original agreement, GATT 1947. In addition to the GATT, many other agreements have been negotiated, some of which have been able to steal the lime-light of late. The most controversial of these, and therefore the most notorious, are the General Agreement on Trade in Services (GATS), the Agreement on Trade-Related Investment Measures (TRIMS), and the Agreement on Trade-Related Aspects of Intellectual Property Rights (TRIPS). As said, the economies in the First World are becoming increasingly service oriented, and in recognition of this, the WTO has negotiated GATS, which aims to achieve the equivalent for services of what the GATT did for goods. TRIPS introduces rules and regulations with respect to patent rights, copyrights, trademarks, and industrial designs. TRIMS ostensibly aims to set rules for investors in foreign countries, although it has been criticized for being more about the rights of investors themselves.

The GATT took almost a half century to write and incor-porates the outcome of a string of negotiations, each stage referred to as a "round." Rounds are usually named after their location, with the exception of two that took place in Geneva, which, in order to avoid confusion, were named after prominent politicians. The two persons honoured thus far have both been American, a trade bureaucrat by the name of Douglas Dillon and President John F. Kennedy. Ministerial committees provide trade delegates with the opportunity to decide which topics will be negotiated in the upcoming round. With the exception of the Seattle Summit, and to a lesser degree the one in Doha, Qatar, these meetings generally go unnoticed and generate little news beyond the business pages. The rounds themselves have ᴢen marked by an increase in length. The first few rounds were only a few months long, whereas the more recent ones lasted years. The eighth round, which led to the establishment of the WTO, was held in Punta del Este, Uruguay, and lasted from 1986 to 1994 for a total of eight years. After the Qatar ministerial meeting, the ninth round is now certain to go ahead, the location of which has yet to be determined.

The Ground Rules of the WTO

The WTO overrules all other trade agreements, and it is indicative of its flexibility that regional trade agreements, such as the North American Free Trade Agreement (NAFTA) and the European Union (EU), are allowed to coexist within its mandate. The preferences that a regional agreement bestows upon its members obviously contravene the spirit of global free trade that the WTO stands for. This raises one of the most important principles underlying the multilateral agreement that is the GATT, that of equal treatment. In order to join the WTO, a country has to abide by the Most Favoured Nation (MFN) principle, which stipulates that a country has to treat all other countries equally (the "principle of non-discrimination" in the words of the GATT). This means, in a rather roundabout way, that when you play favourites with one country, you have to play favourites with all. In that sense, the MFN status almost means the direct opposite of what it states. When everybody is the most favourite, no one is. It is like having ten provinces all claiming to have "distinct society" status. Relatedly, the national treatment clause specifies that a government must treat foreign goods the same way as domestic ones, but this only includes goods and not services. The primary aim of this rule is to ensure that governments do not discriminate against exports when purchasing goods. Together, these two clauses guarantee equal treatment of foreign products both inside and outside of the country.

Two additional principles that underlie the GATT are those of reciprocity and transparency. Reciprocity stipulates that once a country lowers tariffs on imports from country A, that country is obliged to return the favour. This may seem self-evident but is not always the case. This kind of lopsided arrangement is precisely what occurred under the Ottawa Agreements during the Depression. Some countries raised their tariffs on manufactured goods originating in Great Britain in order to protect their own infant industries, whereas Great Britain felt confident its industries could survive without tariffs. Similarly, Canada erected tariff walls to keep out industrial goods from Great Britain, but imposed no such penalties on industrial goods from Australia.

The principle of transparency prohibits countries from engaging in barriers to trade that are hidden, such as export quotas. If they do participate in such unsavoury practices they are, under the GATT, compelled to eventually turn them into tariffs. The bottom line is that the WTO wants barriers to trade to be easily identified, as are tariffs, and once they have been exposed (are transparent), seeks their elimination.

A tariff is simply a tax applied on goods or services, and is implemented primarily to protect domestic industries. Tariffs, or duties as they are sometimes referred to, are effective because they raise the prices of imported products and render them less competitive. Tariffs may also be applied to exports, but this happens less frequently, as when a country seeks to keep certain items, such as rare artifacts, within its borders. In other instances, export tariffs amount to no more than a tax grab. An example of this is the export tariff applied by the Iranian government to quality carpets. Tariffs have been applied by nation states for as long as they have existed and by city states before that. And despite concerted efforts by trade organizations around the world to get rid of them, they are likely be around for some time.

While the GATT has been quite successful in lowering tariffs, it has been less so in lowering hidden barriers to trade. In the language of trade negotiators, these barriers are referred to as non-tariff barriers (NTBs), the most notorious of which are voluntary export restraints (VERs). The United States has repeatedly attempted to place a duty on Canadian imports of softwood lumber, arguing that low stumpage fees are a form of subsidy. During the 1996 negotiations, in order to avoid such a duty, Canada "volunteered" to limit the amount of softwood it would export to the United States. Similar tactics have been used to convince the Japanese automobile industry to contain its exports. The United States has also been known to pressure Third World countries into restricting the amount of clothing they are able to export. The United States is notorious for the imperiousness with which it conducts itself in these trade talks. Peter Murphy, the chief negotiator for the Americans in the Canada US Free Trade Agreement, cut his teeth working for the US textile industry. Canadian journalist Linda McQuaig writes that during negotiations with a Third World country, Murphy would extend an offer of, say, the importation of 100 000 shirts. If the trade delegates sitting across the table did not like the offer, Murphy's subsequent offer would drop to 90 000, then 80 000, and so on.[49] This illustrates that "voluntary" export limits are anything but and allow little discretion to the exporting country.

Subsidies

Another common NTB is subsidies. A subsidy is not a barrier as such, but is considered one just the same, as it effectively keeps out foreign competition. By lowering the cost of production at home, it makes domestic goods artificially competitive both at home and abroad. Subsidies are of two kinds: those targeted at a specific industry or company (for example, the aerospace industry in general or a company such as Bombardier in particular) and those directed at the population in general. Industry-specific subsidies can take many forms: lump sum payments, low- or no-interest loans, loan guarantees, or tax concessions. It is these kinds of subsidies that are particularly shunned by the WTO. Subsidies in commerce are illegal for the same reason as those in amateur sports: They provide an unfair advantage. Athletes who are subsidized by the state, or professionals, have an unfair advantage in that they are able to train more than athletes who need to work to support themselves. Along the same lines, subsidized industries are able to survive with a thinner profit margin than those that rely solely on their own finances. Subsidies are pervasive, and will never be eliminated. This point cannot be overstated. Not only are subsidies demanded by industries that see themselves falling behind foreign competitors, but they are also offered by governments hoping to entice new industries. They range from huge subsidies given to the agricultural industries to tax concessions offered to car plants in Ontario, Michigan, and Alabama. Sometimes, requests remain unanswered, such as when Canadian NHL teams pleaded for help from the government because of the low Canadian dollar. But just as often, requests are met. After the terrorist attack on the World Trade Center, the airline industry suffered losses worldwide and the American government channelled billions of dollars into its own carriers. Canadian farmers are continually clamouring for assistance, and in 2002 the federal and provincial governments responded with a $8.2 billion aid package.

Interestingly, the WTO condones subsidies aimed at the general public, which include all programs generally associated with the welfare state: health, education, pensions, employment insurance, and social assistance, as well as infrastructure or transfer payments that affect regions, such as equalization payments in Canada or the EU. Welfare state programs obviously increase the competitiveness of a workforce, and as such, it is surprising that countries do not take more advantage of them. They are both legal and effective. For example, a recent study shows that in the year 2000 it cost an additional US $930 to produce a car in the United States because of private health insurance.[50] These costs are sidestepped with a publicly funded system, which partially explains why so many auto manufacturers have chosen to locate in Southern Ontario.

Subsidies are, of course, in the eye of the beholder, and many a trade dispute has been fought over an issue where it was not entirely clear what constituted a subsidy. The ongoing problem with softwood lumber is a case in point. American lumber producers argue that low stumpage fees in Canada are tantamount to a subsidy. American forests in the South were part of a make-work project under the New Deal during the Depression. American sports arenas are frequently paid for by municipalities hoping to attract professional sports teams. The American aerospace industry has greatly benefited from military subsidies. It is worthwhile noting that the WTO has an obvious bias towards government subsidies, whereas private subsidies are generally ignored. If a corporation directs millions of dollars into the development of a product, it is called an investment; if a government does the same, it is considered a subsidy. For example, American-produced passengers cars are often sold at a loss, subsidized by the profits made from trucks and sport-utility vehicles.[51] Technically speaking, this means these cars are dumped, but as said, the WTO seems to pay less attention to what private companies do.

There are additional, less commonly used, NTBs. The misuse of customs regulation is a practice that occurs infrequently, primarily because it so blatantly protectionist and could have no other possible motive than keeping imports out. This occurred, for instance, when US meat inspectors deliberately delayed the processing of Canadian beef at their border. A more common non-tariff barrier is the sometimes arbitrary application of technical standards. Often, the intended aim of this process is to force companies to locate production in the same place as their market, as when the Canadian corporation Bombardier built a plant in Great Britain rather than put up with constant harassment about standards. At other times, technical standards have been used to keep products out. Environmental standards are often misused in this way, and we will discuss this in some detail in the following chapter, which takes a look at some case studies. Either way, technical standards impede trade and are not looked upon kindly by the WTO.

Dumping and Countervailing Measures

When a product is sold in another country for a lower price than in the domestic market, or a lower price than the cost of production, it is considered to be dumped. To sell a product for less than cost may not seem like a very intelligent business practice, but this tactic is often used effectively in order to gain a foothold in the market. When Microsoft gives away its browser, we know it is not out of the goodness of its collective heart, but to gain market share. Once market share has success-fully been secured, and competitors have been greatly weak-ened or eliminated, the producer is then free to raise prices. If it is shown that a country is in fact engaging in dumping, the affected country can impose a duty known as anti-dumping duty. If the product in question is more competitive because of a government subsidy, the affected country can apply a tariff called a countervailing duty. Countervailing and anti-dumping duties are essentially the same thing; it is only the source of the subsidy that differs. In the case of countervailing duties the subsidy is public, in anti-dumping duties, private.

Five Reasons Why the WTO Is Not Likely to Be the Next World Government

The above illustrates that the WTO had to surmount many obstacles to become established. But this only hints at the number of problems that lay in the way of a smooth-functioning trading system. All this conflict reveals that the organization is being pulled in many policy directions. Disagreement and strife greatly undermine the power of the organization and suggest it need not be feared. The reasons for this are many, and can best be summarized in the following five points.

1) Lack of Enthusiasm

Before a proper appraisal of the WTO can be conducted, we must ask why countries join the organization in the first place and why what they hope to get out of it. The obvious answer is to promote free trade, but that glosses over the considerable dissension that exists among the organization's members. As the last two ministerial meetings in Seattle and Oman have shown, participating countries find it difficult to decide which topics should be included in the next round, let alone resolve those issues. If all signs pointed in the same direction, then such problems would obviously not arise. Everybody would agree that free trade is a wonderful thing, and that would be that—nice and simple. But we know that free trade is anything but, making one suspect that not all countries are of the same mind.

It is important to take into consideration that much disagreement exists around the world, as well as within individual countries, about the desirability of free trade. It is not uncommon to envision the WTO as a supranational institution capable of overriding the sovereignty of individual governments. But if this were the case, few countries would join. This raises an interesting question: Why, in light of all this disagreement, do countries even bother to join? There are several answers to this question. A large number of industrial countries have joined in hope of having at least some influence over the organization's agenda. Others have joined because of peer pressure, and are afraid they might be kept out of potentially lucrative markets if they do not. And still others have joined anticipating that the WTO will provide a counterbalance to the whims of the more powerful industrial countries, the United States in particular. Canada is a perfect example of this, and its strong support for free trade is based on very practical considerations. Canada has learned from past experiences that the United States can quickly turn protectionist, and it has signed several free trade agreements in hope of stopping its only contiguous neighbour from arbitrarily closing its borders. Yet things have not diverged that much from the past: Neither the establishment of NAFTA nor the WTO has been effective in containing America's protectionist urges. The ongoing struggle over softwood lumber well illustrates this point.

In general the majority of industrial countries, and in particular Europe and Japan, are less enthusiastic about free trade than the United States and Canada. Some of these countries have joined because they wager it is better than the alternative: an anarchic system where the United States dominates. With the WTO, there is at least some hope of establishing ground rules and containing power imbalances. As we have seen, the agenda of the WTO is essentially steeped in Anglo-Saxon history and ideology, and not all countries necessarily subscribe to these ideas with the same enthusiasm as do Great Britain, the United States, and Canada. Other countries may not exactly oppose free trade but have reservations about the way it is currently implemented. In other words, support for free trade in these countries can range from skeptical to tepid to underwhelming.

The current trade agenda is part of what is sometimes referred to as the Washington Consensus, which reveals an obvious American bias. That fact alone makes many other countries suspicious of the whole endeavour. In a world where anti-American sentiment is plentiful, we can expect a healthy mistrust of anything the United States supports. In short, few countries savour another global institution dominated by the United States.

2) Poor Countries Have Little to Gain

What is true for the less powerful industrial countries, such as Canada, is even more so for the Third World. We have seen that the United States has enough influence over the WTO to be able to structure the rules to its own advantage. This primarily involves pushing activities at which it is clearly superior (high-tech and services) while ignoring those at which it is less competitive (primarily agriculture, horticulture, and textiles). In poor countries, where the majority of the population continues to be involved in subsistence farming, these policies find little resonance. Such countries have few productive facilities in the service sector and are unlikely to gain from these new agreements. And, as the example of drug or seed patents well illustrates, poor countries are likely to suffer from their implementation. In one respect, the reasons that Third World countries have joined the WTO are similar to those of the First World countries: potential access to markets, and fear of what it might mean not to be a member. Another reason, this one not being applicable to First World countries, is that some Third World countries have been cajoled to join the WTO by the World Bank or the IMF through strings that are attached to loans. Ideology also plays a role here. Many Third World economists are trained at American universities and bring back with them a souvenir: the ideology of free trade.

3) Domestic Conflict

Opposition to free trade originates not only in countries unlikely to benefit from it, but also in countries that generally support it. Even countries with deep roots in the ideology of free trade are home to industries that oppose it, sometimes vigorously so. Rarely do industries injured by free trade bravely swallow their free market medicine in the name of the common good. They fight back, and often with government on their side. While the United States has publicly, and often boastingly, espoused free trade, it has in fact intervened in the free market as much, if not more, than anyone. From the American Revolution onwards, up to and including the Depression, the United States became increasingly protectionist. While the official policy has changed considerably towards free trade since that time, underlying protectionist sentiments linger and are able to strike with considerable force. And so it is to this day: If and when the United States feels that one of its own is threatened, it will do everything in its power to protect it. This rather high-handed approach has resulted in a flood of complaints against American trade practices. A November 2001 article in *The Globe and Mail* documents that 70 percent of WTO complaints in the previous two years were lodged against the United States.[52] Bruce Little summarized this attitude as follows: "A level playing field is one on which Americans win, because, as every American knows in his bones, Americans always win a fair fight. If they lose, the fight is, by definition, unfair."[53]

To be honest, most countries would behave in a similar fashion if they were in the position to do so. What makes the United States different is that it can do as it pleases and get away with it. In other words, America's inconsistency towards open markets is justified not by logic but by political and economical clout. Canada has also caved in to demands from the wheat and dairy industries to be excluded from current trade agreements. In order to protect domestic producers, tariffs on clothing and textiles remain high. And Canada continues to subsidize a variety of industries, a series of loan guarantees to Bombardier being an example. Of course, self-interest is not the exclusive province of the United States or Canada, and other countries think and act along similar lines. But it is primarily the rich countries that are able to effectively enforce this self-interest, leaving the Third World with few advantages from free trade.

Inconsistencies are apparent not only within countries but also within business groups. Ideology appears to play an important role in the support for free trade among some interest groups, even if those interests are not served all that well by free trade. In Canada, corporations are represented by the BCNI (the Business Council on National Issues, recently renamed the CCCE [the Canadian Council of Chief Executives]), a lobby group headed by Thomas d'Aquino. According to Peter Newman, the CCCE is the most influential and economically powerful interest group in the country. It is also a fervent supporter of free trade. Thomas d'Aquino turned out to be one of the most visible and ardent supporters of the Canada US Free Trade Agreement in the late 1980s. It is somewhat perplexing, then, that many of the CCCE's members operate in markets that are not open to international competition. According to William Thorsell, 42 percent of CCCE members operate in a protected market.[54] In Canada, the telecommunications industries and airlines, as well as financial services, would likely suffer if markets were opened to foreign competitors. Members of the CCCE act as though they know it, and many have lobbied aggressively to keep foreign corporations out. The chartered banks in

Canada, for example, have a virtual monopoly in this country. Foreign entrants would likely translate into considerable losses for Canadian banks (and probably better services for Canadian customers). Again, here we have an organization that puts on a brave face when it comes to public support of free trade, yet when it comes to actual behaviour, allows considerable latitude within its ranks. The fact that many industries in pro–free trade countries fail to support open markets means that free trade is more difficult for governments to enforce. Such breaches also tarnish the image of free trade and impair the authority of an organization like the WTO.

4) Size Matters
The late Dalton Camp, a long-time columnist for the *Toronto Star*, described the WTO as "the most powerful, influential, and feared unelected body in the universe since Thomas de Torquemada headed up the Spanish Inquisition."[55] This is most certainly nonsense, but such hyperbole has struck a chord with many anti–free traders. If power is the realization of intended ends, the evidence shows that the WTO is rather an ineffective organization. First, let us look at the often-made claim that free trade exists to enrich corporations. There is little doubt that corporate interests have considerable influence on governments in all industrial countries. But corporations can only lobby their governments and hope their interests are represented at negotiations. Often they do so to great effect, but there is no direct transmission of power from corporations to the WTO. For one, only government officials represent their countries at negotiations. Moreover, governments have to answer not only to conflicting corporate

interests but also to voters. This makes it substantially more difficult for any one industry to have its wishes implemented. Another factor that limits the power of the WTO is that it is democratic and has a mandate from all its member countries.[56] And precisely because the WTO is democratic, the United States has decided to put most of its energies into the World Bank and the IMF. The US veto power over decisions made by these institutions makes them significantly more responsive to Washington's demands. In comparison, America's power base in the WTO, one vote in 144, is much more diluted. Furthermore, in comparison with other international organizations, the WTO is small. The World Bank employs 7500 employees; the IMF 2500; the WTO secretariat a comparatively measly 550—no more than a small university in Canada. Even the OECD (Organisation for Economic Co-operation and Development) has more employees, with 2100. In this sense, the WTO's power pales in comparison with that of these other institutions. The WTO is chronically starved for cash and understaffed. It takes well over a year for a complaint to be heard and even longer to get a ruling. Examples of its impotence are common. Europe has ignored a ruling that it cannot boycott North American beef; Japan and Europe steadfastly refuse to dismantle subsidies in agriculture; the United States insists on applying tariffs on Canadian softwood; and Brazil refuses to stop subsidizing its aerospace industry. All these activities are illegal under the GATT, and such a track record is certainly not indicative of a new world government. It seems that with or without trade agreements, countries do as they please. Meanwhile, the WTO stands by and is able to do nothing. Based on the organization's fecklessness, countries are becoming increasingly reluctant to take the legal route. The WTO is still relatively young, only about eight years old, and the next few years will be critical to its reputation. It will have to show that it is able to deal firmly with countries that flout its rules. But if the past is any indication, detractors have little to worry about.

5) Sovereignty

Related to the fear that the WTO is undemocratic and all-powerful is its perceived ability to override the sovereignty of member governments. This view also identifies the WTO as an instrument of multinational corporations. But such fears are, again, unwarranted. The state, just like any other organization, seeks to perpetuate itself and consequently tries to protect its power base. To phrase this observation in the form of a question, Why would any government willingly enter an agreement that threatened to undermine its own power? Well, the short answer is that states are generally not in the habit of doing such things, and it is certainly not the case here. Governments continue to have inordinate power in today's world: They control the law, police, military, movement of people, and a huge portion of the national budget. States enact laws; corporations can only hope governments will write legislation that will benefit them. Governments enforce laws; corporations can only hope to effectively use the legal system to their advantage. And let us not forget, it is governments that negotiate trade deals.

An additional reason not to be overly concerned about the WTO undermining national autonomy is that its strongest member, the United States, is extraordinarily skittish about its sovereignty. Americans are notoriously reluctant to take orders from anyone. It simply does not make sense that such a country would sign an agreement that could potentially imperil its authority. Examples abound of agreements that the United States has obdurately refused to sign because of concerns about sovereignty. The Kyoto Protocol, which establishes baseline reductions in greenhouse gases, is only the most recent and glaring example of this. Many attribute this retrograde attitude to the current right-wing government, but this aversion to signing international agreements has a long history. In December 1997, under the Clinton administration, the United States refused to sign the Ottawa Treaty on the Elimination of Land Mines. The United States also stands alone in refusing to sign a number of agreements that have to do with military security: the 1972 Biological and Toxic Weapons Convention, the 1972 Anti–Ballistic Missile Treaty, as well as a treaty to stop nuclear testing. The United States also has refused to back a United Nations plan for a permanent international criminal court to prosecute war criminals. As we saw, the United States failed to ratify the charter that would have launched the ITO, and going back even further, it declined to sign on to the League of Nations, the forerunner of the United Nations. This list is by no means exhaustive, yet it strongly suggests that the most powerful country in the world is not likely to sign away its autonomy. Naturally, other countries have similar concerns. China, for example, has traditionally been loath to do what others tell it. It has shot missiles at Taiwan, executed its criminals on a large scale, run tanks over its own demonstrators, and attacked spy planes it considered to be in its territory. Again, these actions are not indicative of a country that would freely abandon its sovereignty.

Closed Trade

When all is said and done, there is actually very little free trade going on; in short, there are too many exceptions. Producers of agricultural products and textiles in the Third World have been offered little but closed borders by the First World (this issue is discussed in more detail in chapter 9). Knowledge industries are able to protect themselves to the point of monopoly. The existence of regional trade agreements, such as the EU and NAFTA, means that the Most Favoured Nation status is essentially meaningless.

Another significant sector of the economy that the WTO has explicitly chosen to ignore is military expenditure. Funding for the military, particularly in the United States, has translated into huge subsidies for many of its industries. In 1998, the United States spent US $265 billion on defence, which amounted to just over 3 percent of GDP (in contrast, Canada spends marginally more than 1 percent). Because of the terrorist attacks, this figure is projected to increase to a whopping US $379 billion in 2003. This kind of money has countless benefits for domestic industries. For one, in 1998 the United States sold US $7.1 billion of weapons abroad, almost one-third of the global total. But this pales in comparison with local industries that benefit from lucrative military contracts. In 1996, Lockheed Martin received US $12 billion, McDonnell Douglas US $10 billion, General Motors US $3.2 billion, and Boeing US $1.7 billion in defence contracts. And the list goes on: AT&T, Texas Instruments, Black and Decker, Exxon, all received contracts in 1996 of around half a billion dollars each. Even Noam Chomsky's employer, the Massachusetts Institute of Technology, is a major recipient of military funding. Given the battles that have ensued from mere loan guarantees, the awarding of such profitable contracts is highly questionable. Like all subsidies, these have resulted in American industries being unfairly competitive. The aerospace industry, a major export for the United States, owes much of its success to decades of profligate military subsidies. This makes it all the harder for foreign corporations, such as Airbus in Europe, to compete, let alone for other competitors to enter the market from scratch.

Military expenditures in the United States have resulted in a unique kind of government intervention. Some people have accused Reagan, the great conservative, of practising what they refer to as military Keynesianism. Rather than spending billions on the poor, public health, or education, Reagan spent it on the military. Had he used similar subsidies to directly support private industry, it clearly would have been illegal. Supporters of military spending contend it would be imprudent to prohibit subsidies on the basis that it would imperil national security. But the same thing could be said about food production, or, for that matter, any industry. Moreover, if the WTO is so enthusiastic about trade and peace, as it claims on its Web page, why does it not make military subsidies illegal and discourage the manufacture of weapons in the first place?

Conclusion

Adam Smith was fascinated by the way the division of labour led to greater efficiencies in the economy. One could similarly argue that any organization works better once it specializes. Some organizations fight for less government, some for the homeless, some for civil liberties. And the list goes on: against drunk drivers, for the legalization of drugs, against a freeway, for a park. The WTO happens to advocate free trade and we should not expect it to start fighting to save the environment, much the same way we would not expect Greenpeace to champion free trade. This is not to say that the WTO and Greenpeace are equally influential. Power largely depends on the company one keeps, and the WTO does keep powerful friends indeed. The main source of its power comes from having interests that coincide with those of governments and corporations, two of the more powerful institutional actors in contemporary society. Unfortunately, the WTO perpetuates contemporary imbalances in global power rather than transcends them, and so the First World, particularly the United States, has much more influence over the WTO's agenda than do Third World countries.

This, however, by no means translates into absolute power either for business, government, or the WTO. Comparisons with the Spanish Inquisition border on the fantastic. Institutions rarely achieve that kind of autonomy. If it does happen, obsession is free to run wild. In a classic analysis of the SS, the German secret police during the Second World War, Everett Hughes concludes that the organization grew so corrupt because it had no one to answer to.[57] Every organization, of course, strives for exactly that kind of independence, but, fortunately, few are ever able to achieve it. The WTO most definitely falls into the latter category. First, the WTO is accountable to its members, who fund it. Second, and related to this first point, the WTO indirectly has to answer to the citizens of the countries it represents. These democratic checks go a long way towards containing the power of the institution. Third, the WTO is susceptible to public opinion, and it is already suffering from more than its fair share of bad press. The WTO is acutely aware of the hordes of naysayers just waiting in the wings for it to slip up. That kind of public scrutiny has meant that the WTO has had to be extra careful about how it conducts itself.

The best way to assess how effective the WTO and other trade agreements have been is to compare their past performance with their stated objectives. Let us imagine for a minute how the global economy would be structured if free traders were able to realize their dreams. In such a world, a firm would be able to consolidate its production in one location and, from there, supply the rest of the world. In the interest of efficiency, Japan could produce all its vehicles at home rather than setting up branch plants around the world. The same would be true for Bombardier; it could easily service the world market from its home base in Canada. But firms are coerced into building branch plants by governments that want jobs in their jurisdictions. No trade organization has been able to stop these practices, highlighting how difficult it is to enforce free trade. In a world of free trade, there would be no marketing boards for dairy products in Canada and no subsidies to the military. Neither would Brazil and Canada be able to provide loan guarantees to their aerospace industries. Lumber from Canada would flow freely across the American border, and Europe would buy Canadian and American beef injected with growth hormones. The fact that none of these scenarios is taking place greatly calls into question the reality of free trade and the power of the WTO. As the history of free trade demonstrates, there is a litany of issues that has divided countries and industries for decades, and these disagreements are likely to persist and cause divisions well into the future.

An equitable system of free trade is clearly more challenging to enforce than first appears. Canada is typical of how countries exhibit a lackadaisical attitude towards the topic. Whereas Canada firmly supports a global system of trade, it frequently breaks the rules. In the following chapter, we are going to find out how countries try to wriggle out of the straitjacket that is free trade when it does not meet their immediate objectives.

7

The first requisite of liberty is order.
—GEORG WILHELM HEGEL

CASE STUDIES: TRADE, THE ENVIRONMENT, AND NATIONAL SOVEREIGNTY

THE BEST WAY TO ILLUSTRATE some of the complications that arise from free trade is through the examination of case studies. Making trade rules that are both fair and effective is much harder to achieve than first appears, and given the wide variety of interests involved, may well be impossible. On top of the list of contentious issues is without a doubt that of the environment (environment will be used in its broadest sense here and include health standards that are associated with food additives and pesticides). Those who oppose free trade often do so on the basis that agreements pay too little attention to the environment. On the other hand, trade organizations have been reluctant to include provisions for the environment because they are afraid they will be used as a pretext to implement non-tariff barriers. The tension between the environment and trade is one that has proven to be difficult to reconcile, and consequently the WTO has tried to stay clear of the issue. But this has been to no avail. Many of the most publicized cases to come before the WTO or NAFTA tribunal—tuna/dolphins, sea turtles, the gasoline additive MMT—have touched on the environment. Another issue that pervades these cases, and one that is also a major concern among those who oppose free trade, is, as we have seen, national sovereignty. Detractors charge that the WTO effectively acts like a world government, able to override decisions made by national governments. Free trade, the environment, and national sovereignty are all emotional issues in their own right, and when they come together, as they often do, the result can be controversial.

The WTO—like the GATT before it—opposes an environmental clause because it believes that governments would abuse it, and as we shall see, that reluctance is well placed. An example of the arbitrary use of health standards involved the prohibition of Canadian salmon in Australia. In 1975, Australia implemented a ban on imported salmon that was neither heat treated nor canned. On that basis, fresh, frozen, and chilled salmon from Canada was kept from entering Australia, a ban that lasted for over twenty years. In 1997, Canada appealed the law, arguing that there were no known negative health effects associated with uncooked salmon and that the ban unfairly penalized British Columbia producers. Canada won the case, a decision that was good for Canadian fishers but not Australian sovereignty. Proponents of the latter might argue that a country should be able to do whatever it pleases, much the same way that an individual cannot be forced to buy a product, and if Australia chooses not to import Canadian salmon, so be it. It is difficult not to have some sympathy with this view, but in the end, allowing such discretion would surely open the floodgates to non-tariff barriers.

Let us take this one step further and speculate how an environmental provision might be exploited. The United States lumber industry has long resorted to every trick in the book in order to stop more competitive Canadian imports from coming across its borders. If an environmental provision were available, it is entirely conceivable that the United States would use it to justify boycotting Canadian lumber. As some European environmental groups have already done, Americans could argue that Canada engages in destructive activities such as clear-cutting, including that of original rain forests. While environmentalists might applaud such a decision, it could devastate the Canadian, and particularly the British Columbian, economy. American logging practices may not be any more environmentally friendly than Canadian ones, but that is to miss the point. The overarching problem is that if a country had the option of using an environmental clause to protect local industry, it would likely do so at every opportunity. Former US president Jimmy Carter recently made an argument that reveals the vulnerability of such a clause. He fears that because of Canada's lower lumber prices "many [American] landowners cannot afford to invest in reforestation and forest maintenance, and the consequence will be land that is barren or converted to other uses."[58] In other words, Americans cannot compete. But rather than suggest giving up the industry, which is the logical free market solution, Carter urges tariffs on Canadian lumber imports.

What Carter is really saying in a roundabout way is that he, being a woodland owner himself, is unable to compete and wants some help from the government so he can. Could this tariff be justified on environmental grounds? Whatever the answer, this case should prove to be an instructive lesson for those who support environmental regulation as part of trade agreements.

Ironically, the WTO opposes an environmental clause for precisely the same reason as its opponents: Trade organizations are afraid to encroach on the sovereignty of governments, or even to be seen encouraging one country to dictate environmental policy to another. The crux of the problem is that when the environment and national sovereignty are pitted against each other, both issues traditionally supported by the left, one has to give. The tuna/dolphin case reveals this contradiction. The United States passed legislation prohibiting American fishers from using nets that inadvertently trapped and slaughtered dolphins. Since this was strictly a domestic matter, the WTO offered no opinion. Soon after, the United States expanded the law to include imports, effectively barring tuna from countries that continued to use nets harmful to dolphins. Mexico, of the countries affected, opposed this law and took the case to the GATT in 1991. The GATT sided with Mexico, arguing that American and Mexican tuna were similar products, and how they were procured was inconsequential. By preferring a domestic product to an identical imported product, the Americans had violated the non-discrimination clause of the GATT. More important, the decision signalled to the United States that it could not impose its own environmental standards on other countries. The GATT dispute panel explicitly highlighted the importance of Mexico's sovereignty, and by not forcing Mexico to adopt America's environmental policies, was careful to avoid stepping on anyone's jurisdictional toes. The outcome of this case, then, might have been a blow to those who support the environment but not to those who champion national sovereignty, and the case illustrates that both objectives are not always attainable.

MMT

One of the most publicized cases, and the one most frequently invoked by the left to illustrate how free trade agreements undermine national sovereignty, is that of the gasoline additive MMT.[59] This case features the Canadian government and Ethyl Corporation of Virginia, the sole producer of MMT in North America. Introduced as an alternative to lead in the mid-1970s, MMT enhances octane count in gasoline. Health concerns similar to those about lead are associated with this product, and it is suspected that it may be a neurotoxin. The controversy over the health effects of MMT, like many environmental issues, is far from settled, and the scientific debate about its merits and demerits is ongoing. Given its tentative health status, MMT has variously been legal and illegal throughout North America. It was banned in the United States for a period of seventeen years, and is currently illegal in several states, including California.

But that is not the only reason why MMT is controversial. Automakers disapprove of it because it allegedly gums up emission-control devices, costing the industry millions of dollars in warranty replacements. Environmental groups and the automobile industry are natural allies in this cause and have come together to argue that MMT, by reducing the effectiveness of pollution-control devices, worsens air pollution. The only interest group that supports the use of MMT is the oil industry, primarily because it is the least expensive option available to refineries. To switch to an alternative octane enhancer would cost the Canadian oil industry an initial capital outlay of $115 million and an additional $50 million a year to maintain. The oil companies obviously would prefer to forgo these costs, and they have fought tooth and nail to keep MMT legal. This conflict of interests has pitted some of the largest industries in the country against one another and resulted in some of the most intensive lobbying that Ottawa has seen in years.

Predictably, interests can also be broken down by region. Ontario, the heart of the Canadian auto industry, sided with the ban as expected, since its automakers had to absorb the extra costs associated with pollution-control devices. But in this stance, Ontario was in the minority. Eight provincial governments, including those of Alberta and Quebec, came out and opposed Bill C-29, the federal legislation proposed to curtail the use of MMT.

The federal government was naturally torn between these powerful interests, so in order not to offend anyone, the government proscribed the importation and interprovincial transport of MMT rather than outright prohibit its use. But Ethyl Corporation would have none of this, and predictably challenged this watered-down version of the law under NAFTA. It argued that the law made little sense, since Ethyl Corporation was free to produce and market MMT within Canada by establishing a plant in each of the provinces.[60]

Furthermore, Ethyl Corporation already owned and operated a mixing plant in Ontario, which would remain perfectly legal under the new bill. Under Chapter 11 of NAFTA, Ethyl Corporation sued the Canadian government for $350 million for expropriation of profits, although the two sides eventually settled out of court for $19 million. But the American corporation was not the only party unsatisfied with the bill. The Alberta government wrote that it was "deeply troubled by the unilateral manner" in which the federal government had outlawed transportation of MMT, and challenged the bill under Canada's Internal Trade Agreement. A Canadian court agreed with the provinces, and Bill C-29 was declared illegal before the case ever went to the NAFTA tribunal. In other words, the law would not have survived even if Ethyl Corporation had never taken issue with it.

As previously stated, this case is often invoked as evidence of how corporations are able to effectively override the sovereignty of national governments. On closer examination, however, the challenge by Ethyl Corporation arose because the federal government was too pusillanimous to ban MMT outright (as some American states have done) and instead introduced a law that it hoped would accommodate the wishes of various industrial and environmental groups. In the end, it failed to satisfy anyone, and it is difficult to imagine how the authors of the bill speculated it would do otherwise. Why such a careless law was introduced in the first place remains a mystery. Some have speculated that the intended effect was for Ethyl Corporation to establish branch plants in Canada, but that would have made little sense, as such arrangements are clearly illegal under the Canada US Free

Trade Agreement. Others, including Ethyl Corporation itself, have put forward the idea that the bill amounted to a blatant act of protectionism and was instigated by the local corn industry. Evidence for either of these points, however, is lacking.

Neville Nankivell has wisely suggested that the federal government should have appointed a commission made up of independent scientists to study the problem, the findings of which would then have been binding on the various parties.[61] A study that comprehensively examined evidence would have allowed lawmakers, as well as the interested public, to weigh the different points of the debate. Opinions like "small amounts of manganese are not harmful to human health," disseminated by the oil industry, fail to inspire much confidence. An independent inquiry would have assured that a more decisive law could have been legislated, one that either banned or permitted use of the substance.

Furthermore, critics pointed out long before the bill was ever passed that it would not have stood up to a court challenge under NAFTA, as it discriminated against imports. An article in *The Financial Post,* which appeared near the end of 1995 (the Manganese-Based Fuel Additives Act was not passed until 1996), presciently stated that the proposed law would not only be an easy target for Ethyl Corporation but also for the provinces, as it presented "an unconstitutional infringement" on provincial rights.[62]

The very important point to be gleaned from this case is that, rather than blame environmental problems on supranational trade organizations or powerful corporations, Canadians would be better advised to look at their own government and incompetent law-making. Even without any trade agreement in place, MMT would still be legal in Canada. The whole debate can be better understood as a conflict between the automobile and oil industries. It can be understood better still through the lens of regionalism, in which Ontario, the heart of the auto industry, saw its interests pitted against those of the other provinces. One can only guess that Ottawa rejected an outright ban of MMT because it was afraid of the uproar this would cause among the provinces, particularly Alberta. The federal government attempted to pre-empt such dissent with the introduction of Bill C-29, yet it proved satisfactory to no one: neither the auto industry, nor the oil industry, nor environmentalists. This is not the only case where the federal government attempted to pass legislation that blatantly contravened trade laws. In 1995, a year previous to the passing of the MMT legislation, the federal government attempted to pass a law that banned the export of PCBs (so it could incinerate them in Canada). The equally weak legislation met a similar fate as the MMT bill. All this does not give one too much confidence in our lawmakers, particularly when it comes to Bill C-32, the anti-terrorist bill.

Unfortunately, those who oppose free trade, particularly those in Canada, have used the MMT case as an exemplar of forced trade, where a private corporation successfully contested the sovereignty of a government. "If NAFTA did not exist, MMT would still be banned in Canada"[63] pretty much summarizes the consensus on the left in Canada. But, as we have just learned, MMT was never banned in Canada, meaning this case, a favourite to illustrate the evils of free trade, is built on easily discreditable claims.

Asbestos

The asbestos dispute is similar to the MMT case in that there is no conclusive scientific evidence that either establishes or refutes the safety of the product. This case also illustrates how the free trade agenda is often driven by corporate interests, in this instance the $224 million asbestos industry in Quebec. Moreover, it reveals that corporate interests are not always able to get what they want. Canada is the second-largest producer of asbestos in the world, but for well-known health reasons, that market has been steadily shrinking in recent decades. As a consequence, the industry has already been hit hard, and it has been estimated that an outright ban would affect the lives of another 2500 workers, mostly in Quebec. Nine countries in the EU have already prohibited all types of asbestos, a ban that will include all EU members by 2005. The loss of American and European markets has meant the majority of Canada's asbestos is now destined for the Third World, which has irked some environmentalists.

But this is not where the story ends. The asbestos industry has argued that only some forms of asbestos are in fact harmful. It admits that a specific type of asbestos, one primarily used in the past and comprising amphibole-shaped fibres, is carcinogenic. However, the industry contends that another variant, one made up of serpentine-shaped fibres and in wide use today, is not injurious to human health. The scientific community is divided on this issue, but the data vindicating the product seemed convincing enough for Prime Minister Chrétien to personally call Prime Minister Ricardo Lagos of Chile to ask him, albeit unsuccessfully, to lift his country's ban on asbestos.

This is not the first time that the Canadian government has gone to bat for the asbestos industry. Only a few years ago, France prohibited asbestos and Canada took the case to the WTO. Canada tried to make the case that the ban on asbestos amounted to a technical ban (a non-tariff barrier), but the WTO sided with France and upheld the prohibition. Here we have a case, then, where the WTO did come down on the side of the environment. Most important, national sovereignty won out, and this case demonstrates that the WTO does not, as its opponents are wont to claim, always rule in favour of trade.

Food Protection and the Third World

Europe wants to have more autonomy over food safety and ecological labelling, precisely the kind of issues that environmentalists have lobbied for. Although a laudable goal, this kind of legislation could easily be abused, as the following case makes clear. Europe wants to raise its standards on the amount of aflatoxin, a fungus, allowed in grains, nuts, and dried fruits. If not properly stored, aflatoxin can become toxic, eventually leading to liver cancer in humans. But the risk of dying from aflatoxin is extremely small; the World Bank argues: "The new aflotoxin [sic] standards would reduce health risks by only about 1.4 deaths per billion a year but would cut African exports 64 percent, or $670 million [US] compared with their level under international standards."[64] This raises the question of whether this amounts to a legitimate health concern or is simply a ruse to stop imports. People who champion Third World economic development would likely oppose such a law, as it would directly affect some of the poorest countries on the globe. Opponents would immediately identify the law as just another tactic by the First World to protect its agriculture. Environmentalists, on the other hand, may argue that a country should be able to set whatever health standards it sees fit. But somebody who champions all three—the Third World, the environment, and sovereignty—and there are many on the left who would fall into this category, would be faced with a difficult contradiction here. If countries were allowed to set their own standards, many industries could be unjustly affected. This is particularly hard on countries that depend on agriculture as their primary means of generating income. But to disallow countries to set their own standards means that their sovereignty is jeopardized. There seems to be no easy solution at hand.

Codex

In order to forestall tactics that exploit the environment for competitive advantage, the WTO relies on a series of UN institutions that oversee environmental standards. Health standards are set by three organizations: (1) Codex Alimentarius Commission (often simply referred to as Codex), which governs food standards such as pesticide use; (2) the International Office of Epizootics, which tracks disease among domestic livestock (for example, foot-and-mouth disease); and (3) the Secretariat of the International Plant Protection Convention, which oversees plant matters. Codex was established in 1963, and more than 120 countries have adopted its provisions since. These institutions, particularly Codex, have come under criticism for applying levels of risk that are higher than those of most national bodies.

Codex and the WTO would no doubt defend their stance and contend that these agencies adhere to only the highest standards of safety. And very little evidence exists that would point to the contrary.

The best way to explain the details of this debate is again, by example. Codex has concluded, along with Health Canada and the Food and Drug Administration (FDA) in the United States, that beef injected with bovine growth hormone was safe for human consumption. Despite these findings, the European Community expressed anxiety about possible health risks, and banned use of this substance as far back as 1989. This decision also meant that Europe would no longer buy North American beef. Canada and the United States objected and took their case to the GATT and then the WTO, which decided against Europe. The court based its decision on evidence from Codex. While the WTO prides itself on allowing countries to set their own level of risk when it comes to food substances, it found the outright ban of the bovine growth hormone to be illegal. Europe has failed to abide by the ruling and still refuses to buy North American beef. Here again, there is more to the case than first appears. Under the veneer of health concerns, we may find old-fashioned protectionism. Industry experts believe that the ban by Europe is a technical barrier to trade, pointing to its use of similar products on pigs and chickens. The WTO reached a similar conclusion and found no evidence that the ban amounted to anything other than a trade barrier.

Many people have expressed dismay at the WTO decision, and it has become another popular example to show how the WTO is able to override national sovereignty. To opponents, the solution to this problem is simple: Allow each country to do as it pleases when it comes to health standards, and if it wishes to invoke the precautionary principle, give it the freedom to do so. The much-discussed precautionary principle states that if full or adequate knowledge about a product is lacking, governing bodies should err on the side of caution and postpone use until further information is made available. For instance, given our limited knowledge of genetically modified food, we should prohibit its sale or consumption until studies have established its safety. Each country should be able to invoke the precautionary principle at its own discretion, and ban controversial drugs, food, or whatever it so deems. The other, and less obvious, side of the coin is that this principle would once again be wide open to abuse by countries wanting to protect local industries. For the WTO to condone the use of the precautionary principle would be tantamount to turning a blind eye to all kinds of sanctions and protectionism. One could easily envision use of the principle to include industrial products such as cars, rejected because they failed to meet stringent environmental or safety standards. By establishing global standards, the WTO is merely attempting to impose some type of order that would pre-empt misuse of environmental regulations. And given what we know about how readily and imaginatively countries use these kinds of provisions, the current attitude of the WTO is wholly understandable and can only be deemed rational.

It is quite apparent that both sides in this debate have legitimate concerns. The WTO's concern about trade barriers may be well placed, yet it is also easy to sympathize with governments worried about their population's health. To allow individual countries to invoke the precautionary principle may seem like an easy solution at first, but on closer examination shows itself to be vulnerable to abuse. Another solution would be to have Codex itself abide by the precautionary principle. This might seem like the most obvious route to take, but such a prescription would be much more difficult to achieve in practice. Since the dawn of the modern age, Western societies have worshipped at the altar of progress. At the same time, citizens around the world have grown comfortable with the risks associated with that progress. In the eyes of many, the benefits of technology have far outweighed its risks. Where to draw the line of how much risk we are able to live with—when to invoke the precautionary principle—is not a simple matter to settle. Codex would insist that it already adheres to the precautionary principle, whereas its critics would say it is not cautious enough. In the end, this debate is entirely too subjective; it is impossible to decide where to draw the precautionary line, leaving us no further ahead.

Let us now consider the consequences of the status quo and try to get a sense of where the current standards of Codex may lead. Are they too permissive, too stringent, or just right? Codex has been in existence for around forty years, the WTO for not much longer than half a dozen, and the Canada US Free Trade Agreement and NAFTA for just over twice as long. And to date, there has not been a major environmental or public health calamity, or for that matter even an isolated incident, under Codex's watch. On this basis, detractors can easily be dismissed as a pack of Jeremiahs. Now it is entirely within the realm of possibility that some kind of disaster might occur in the near future, say the next twenty years. The biggest risk that the WTO has taken is that when standards are applied worldwide, a wrong decision could potentially affect the whole globe. Say, for argument's sake, that a food additive sanctioned by Codex caused a global epidemic that could be linked to one thousand deaths. Such a scenario would quickly and completely discredit Codex and the WTO, and the public outcry would assure that power over health standards would swiftly be brought back to the national level. But this, it bears repeating, is pure conjecture, and should be treated as such. That risk exists, but is in all likelihood low.

One of the biggest problems is that risks are often difficult to ascertain. In the case of bovine growth hormone, the additive MMT, or genetically modified food, health effects are not likely to be all that dramatic. If they were, they could easily be measured. In each of these cases, the controversy exists precisely because consequences are difficult to assess, giving both sides ample room to speculate. Without conclusive evidence, it is just as easy to venture that a product is safe as that it is harmful. Evidence that confirms such risks may take decades to establish. In the case of leaded gasoline, not everyone was affected and effects were cumulative rather than immediate. We read or hear about the possible side effects of additives or pesticides, whether in our food, water, or air, on an almost daily basis, and the majority of people have grown inured to this sort of news. If a study were to link the bovine growth hormone to some kind of cancer, public reaction would likely be muted. Canadians realize that such a study might soon be discounted by another one. Studies that condemn chemical additives are commonplace, but few substances ever result in a major epidemic. In the context of the thousands of chemical products that are used on a daily basis, incidents like those related to asbestos, DDT, and PCBs are the rare exception. This is not the place to get into a debate about risk, but despite pervasive concerns about

alleged poisons that are deliberately pumped into our environment, life expectancy in Canada keeps rising and cancer
rates are generally stable (when controlled by age). In short,
there is no evidence that shows the behaviour of either the
WTO or Codex to be particularly reckless.

Environmental groups do, of course, have legitimate
concerns. Debates about the safety of our food are ongoing. By
deciding to enter the fray, the WTO has brought more than
mere opinion to the table. The WTO has appointed itself and
Codex as judge and jury on these matters, which may present
some problems, as the standards for a court are much different
than those of science. Skepticism is encouraged in all scientific endeavours, and a scientist aware of the limitations of her
study is usually better regarded than one who is all too certain.
But there is no room for doubt in court, and the judge or jury
has to reach a definitive decision. Furthermore, with the
WTO at the helm, people are afraid their own governments
have been sidestepped. Most Canadians are aware that Health
Canada regulates food and drugs, but most have probably
never even heard of Codex. The introduction of an unknown
bureaucratic entity somewhere in Europe has understandably
caused some anxiety. Canadians who are worried about
genetically engineered food, the bovine growth hormone, or
pesticides in their food feel that they have fewer opportunities
to make their concerns heard since the establishment of the
WTO. Finding a way to deal with this problem, one that
essentially comes down to issues of democracy, is no easy task.

Day-to-day life can proceed smoothly because people
generally trust their government to oversee an array of
activities. We get on a plane or an elevator, eat a meal in a
restaurant, undergo an operation, or have a drink of water, all

with the confidence that we will not be harmed. This trust can easily be broken, with potentially dire consequences for all parties involved. When a disaster does occur, the onus is immediately on government and regulating bodies to show that they were as vigilant as they could be. The outbreak of mad cow disease in Great Britain or E. coli in Walkerton, Ontario, illustrates the fallout that is likely to occur once this trust has been broken. The British have been understandably nervous about the safety of their food following their experiences with mad cow and foot-and-mouth disease. As a result, they are now skeptical about genetically engineered food. They have become risk averse, as it were, and that can be a problem in a world driven by technology, a world inherently full of risk. In the end, it comes down to the ability to manage that risk, and how much of it the WTO is willing to take. Given the paucity of evidence, it is premature to judge whether the WTO is too permissive or too cautious. Maybe bovine growth hormone or genetically engineered food is not harmful, but maybe some gasoline additives are, and in the rush to liberalize, the WTO could be sowing the seeds of its own demise. But then again, maybe not.

Conclusion

It is unfortunate, but every system needs rules. We may imagine that we live in a free society, but we have rules and regulations for almost any imaginable activity, and we are often the happier for them. Work, building construction, baseball, poker—even crime—seem to work better when they are organized. The same is true of trade; without rules, the system would certainly not function any better. If Australia could simply refuse to buy Canadian salmon or the United States Canadian lumber—whether for environmental reasons or no reason at all—Canadians would surely suffer in the process. On that basis, most Canadians would likely support some type of regulation, which is precisely the aim of the WTO and NAFTA. This is not to defend free trade as an unqualified good, only to emphasize that without rules there would likely be negative consequences for everybody involved.

Some of the decisions just discussed illustrate that the WTO and NAFTA are less hostile to the environment than their critics claim. MMT is banned in several American states, and fewer and fewer countries are using asbestos. The above evidence suggests that when critics lash out at the WTO, they would be better advised to have a go at their local politicians. MMT continues to be legal in Canada only because our government saw no reason to make it otherwise—free trade had nothing to do with this decision. Genetically engineered food is already labelled in some European countries, but Canadian politicians have chosen not to respond to public pressure in the same way. The cases where the WTO has forced trade on countries, such as hormone-injected beef in Europe, are in the minority, and are based on decisions that reflect the majority of scientific evidence, including that of our own Health Canada.

Still, there exists a tension between trade and the environment, one that may be impossible to resolve. Interest groups are best when they specialize, and the WTO—which is after all an interest group, albeit a powerful one—has unwittingly overreached its jurisdiction. The WTO's mission is free trade, but with Codex it has encroached on the domain of environment. Although the WTO has deliberately avoided enforcing environmental standards on governments (such as with the tuna/dolphin case), setting global standards has amounted to the same thing. When the WTO tells a country it cannot impose its own environmental standards on another country, it is protecting the sovereignty of all its members, but it takes the same right away the moment it sets global standards. On the one hand, then, the WTO is correct to enforce a consistent and exacting set of rules with respect to standards. The arbitrary misuse of technical, and particularly environmental, standards continues to be a major obstacle to free trade. On the other hand, the WTO has to be careful not to become too permissive. One wrong decision, and the result could be a public relations nightmare for the WTO. Such an incident could bring about a backlash not only against the WTO itself, but also against the governments that did not demand a more rigorous level of testing.

The above makes clear that the WTO has a difficult job on its hands, maybe even an impossible one. It cannot ignore the environment precisely because countries will use it as a pretext to erect barriers to trade, yet the environment is not its mandate. As an alternative, many people suggest that governments should have the option of deciding what products they want to import. On the surface, this appears to be a commonsensical solution, particularly given the liberal connotation that is associated with "free trade." But such autonomy would easily be exploited, and thereby debilitate free trade. The rules of trade would no longer be enforceable, as countries could reject almost anything—everything from food, to cars, to lumber—based on environmental concerns.

Europe is seeking an amendment to the GATT that would

allow it to invoke the precautionary principle, but given the likelihood of abuse, the WTO is understandably reluctant to include this amendment. And this gets to the heart of the issue, one that may be irresolvable: to separate issues of trade from the environment. The fact is that at times countries do have legitimate concerns about the environment, and at other times such claims only serve as a convenient excuse to block trade. No organization, the WTO included, can legitimately claim to distinguish between the two. In the end, there is no easy solution to this problem. I have learned from discussions in the classroom that most students are strongly in favour of national sovereignty and the environment. When presented with the tuna/dolphin case, most, but not all, continue to adhere to that stance. When asked to consider the aflatoxin case, a large number begin to reconsider their initial position. And when the possibility is raised that the United States could refuse to buy Canadian softwood on environmental grounds, most realize that an environmental clause would be impossible to enforce fairly. In short, they learn that seemingly simple truths like "national sovereignty is sacred" and "the environment must be protected at all costs" do not stand on their own and become inordinately complicated once applied in the real world.

8

> True individual freedom cannot exist without economic
> security and independence. People who are hungry and out
> of a job are the stuff of which dictatorships are made.
> —FRANKLIN D. ROOSEVELT

FREE TRADE AND
THE THIRD WORLD

BASED ON THE LOTTERY THAT IS LIFE, or at least so the story goes,
some countries are naturally better endowed with resources
than others. Some, like Canada, find themselves with vast
tracts of timber, whereas others, like Brazil, may have perfect
conditions for growing coffee. One country's workforce may
be skilled at manufacturing automobiles, another's at producing shirts, and if all engage in trade, according to the theory,
all will be better off. This makes one wonder, why do poor
countries, at least for the most part, continue to be poor? Not
only that, why, as we shall soon see, is this gap widening? The
answer may, ironically, have less to do with free trade than
with too much interference by the West. By trying their best

to ensure that the market system rules supreme in the Third World, the World Bank and the IMF, and to some degree the WTO, might well have made things worse.

The World Bank and the IMF

The two institutions just mentioned, the World Bank and the IMF, are frequently mentioned in the same breath as the WTO, and for good reason: They share a common history. The World Bank and the IMF, and to a lesser degree the WTO, are all part of a monetary framework designed by Britain and the United States around the end of the Second World War.

The World Bank and the IMF are often referred to as the Bretton Woods Twins, and are considered sister institutions in that they fulfill similar roles. Both are located in Washington, DC, which should give some indication of who dominates these institutions. Another clue that hints at the cozy relationship between the US administration and these organizations is that some commentators have come to include the World Bank and the IMF when they refer to Washington (or the Washington Consensus). The World Bank and the IMF are a direct result of the Bretton Woods negotiations, which took place in New Hampshire in 1944. Given the geopolitical climate at the end of the Second World War, it should come as no surprise that only two countries mattered in these negotiations: Great Britain (represented by John Maynard Keynes) and the United States (represented by Harry Dexter White).[65] It was not long, though, before Keynes's vision of the post-war economy faded, while the imprint of the United States grew correspondingly stronger.

After nearly six decades, these institutions are now well integrated into the American world order. With a few exceptions, such as Cuba and North Korea, this vision has been adopted around the world, but, as we shall see, with varying degrees of success or enthusiasm. By default, the free market system has replaced much of the socialist system in what used to be referred to as the Second World, the erstwhile Soviet Union.

The World Bank and the IMF epitomize the relationship between the First and the Third worlds, a system in which political power directly corresponds to economic strength. Being the world's wealthiest nation in such a system, the United States reigns. This hierarchy is explicit within the World Bank and the IMF, as voting strength is directly related to the size of a country's economy. On this basis, the United States effectively has veto power over any decisions these institutions make. Although the IMF has provided assistance to countries in the First World, all World Bank loans (with the exception of a small number in its early days) and the majority of IMF interventions have been in the Third World. And as is often the case in these situations, these monies come with strings attached. It is not altogether surprising that these strings can be traced to Anglo-Saxon ideas about the free market: no social programs, no deficit, low inflation, privatization, and no subsidies, with few allowances for labour or environmental standards. Not only are these policies an integral part of these institutions' ideologies, but they are explicitly practised in what are called the Structural Adjustment Programs (SAP).

World Bank

There is no such institution as the World Bank. It is merely a term of convenience used to describe two related institutions: the IBRD (International Bank for Reconstruction and Development) and the IDA (International Development Association).[66] Both institutions, as well as the IMF and the WTO, are also part of the UN. The World Bank's headquarters is located, as already mentioned, in Washington, DC, with offices in New York, Paris, Geneva, London, and Tokyo.[67] The IBRD, established in 1944, was initially designed, as the name indicates, to provide loans to countries rebuilding after the war. As a matter of fact, the first (and largest ever) loan made by the bank went to France in 1947. IBRD loans are usually long term and have to be repaid, after an initial five-year grace period, at market interest rates. The other half of the bank, the IDA, was established in 1960. Loans by the IDA are given on much easier terms and primarily geared towards the poorest countries. Unlike IBRD loans, for which market rates prevail, interest rates for IDA loans are usually less than 1 percent. IDA loans also have to be repaid over a period of forty years, compared with fifteen to twenty years for IBRD loans.

The majority of loans by the World Bank are from the IBRD. In 1999, for example, of the US $29 billion lent out by the World Bank, $22 billion, or around three-quarters of the total, originated with the IBRD. The other 25 percent of loans were associated with the IDA. Together these institutions have lent an amount fast approaching half a trillion dollars since their inception, a tidy sum, but one that still greatly underestimates the power of the World Bank. When the

World Bank first lends money to a Third World country, the loan serves as a signal to private investors that the country is a safe haven for investment. In 1998, of the long-term debt owed by the Third World (in contrast with the short-term debt that is the bailiwick of the IMF), only 16 percent was owed to the World Bank. The other 84 percent was owed to private banks (57 percent) and other governments (27 percent). These figures do not include investments such as foreign direct investment, or FDI (the establishment of branch plants, buying of real estate, etc.). This private/public mix tends to favour public debt as risk increases. For example, 72 percent of South American debt is held in private hands, compared with only 24 percent in equatorial Africa.

Of all the institutions that can trace their origins to the Bretton Woods negotiations, the World Bank was very much Keynes's personal project, and were it not for some intensive lobbying on his part, it would likely not exist today. But the World Bank has drastically veered from its original mandate as Keynes envisioned it. This is generally true for all the Bretton Woods institutions, and Keynes's stamp is now notably less visible in global affairs than domestic ones. This has resulted in the ironic situation where Western countries practise Keynesian economics within their own economies while pushing on the Third World a version of the free market model that they themselves are unable to implement at home.

The World Bank was founded as a non-profit organization but soon turned for profit, and it has long raised its funds on the money markets. At least in terms of profits—it has made billions of dollars for its shareholders—it has been very successful. Given that its mandate is so firmly embedded in the free market ideology, one should not be surprised by this. For the first decade or so after its inception, the World Bank was relatively inactive and lent few funds, but this would change significantly under the governance of Robert S. McNamara. Once the president of the Ford Motor Company, McNamara first received worldwide attention as the American defence secretary, a position in which he gained a considerable amount of notoriety because of his involvement in the Vietnam War. Under McNamara's reign, the World Bank became increasingly aggressive and actively began to seek out projects to fund. Its new mandate became to eradicate poverty, and it was under McNamara's tutelage that the World Bank came into its own. After only a cursory examination of documents published by the World Bank, one quickly realizes that it is McNamara's imprint, and not that of Keynes, that continues to be the central driving force behind the institution. The bank's Web page informs visitors that the institution's mission is "A world free of poverty." Topics like "Development Assistance" make clear the institution's heavy reliance on modernization theory. Whether it has been successful at achieving development (whatever that means) or alleviating poverty is not entirely clear. While relative poverty and economic inequality between the First and Third worlds continued to widen throughout the second half of the twentieth century, absolute poverty around the world decreased.[68] But who or what was responsible for this decrease in absolute poverty is difficult to pinpoint. The bank usually likes to take credit for this improvement, but it could just as easily be linked to a number of other factors, including advances in farming or medical technology.

There is considerable evidence, however, that the bank was instrumental in the proliferation of Third World debt. In no way was this due to malice, but rather to two unfortunate and unanticipated developments. One, as part of its mandate, the World Bank attempted to help countries industrialize, which included sponsoring megaprojects such as dams, bridges, and other infrastructure. In order to finance these projects, Third World countries were encouraged to borrow. At first this did not present much of a problem, as in the 1960s and 1970s interest rates were low. But this would soon change. As explained in the introduction, central banks around the world—including the Federal Reserve in the United States, the Bundesbank in West Germany, and the Bank of Canada in Canada—declared war on inflation in the mid-1970s. Their primary policy instrument in this war was high interest rates. This meant that both debts and interest payments everywhere, including those of the Third World, skyrocketed. Put simply, when the Third World was first seduced into going on a borrowing spree money was cheap; when it was time to pay, it was dear.

The second reason for the Third World debt crisis is less well recognized. The West reasoned that if countries wanted to get on the right track towards modernization, they needed to trade more. More trade required that poor countries produce things that could be sold in foreign markets. As it was, these countries were primarily engaged in subsistence agriculture, and Western consumers were not all that interested in buying more rice or corn. Change, for the most part, meant the exploitation of natural resources and a shift from food to cash crops (crops like coffee, which could be sold on the international market rather than consumed locally). An increased reliance on cash crops and natural resources, encouraged by the World Bank throughout the Third World, soon resulted in world markets being flooded with commodities like coffee, cocoa, rubber, and copper. And as any student of economics knows, when there are too many products on the market, prices drop. Things even got worse. In the push to modernize, Third World countries were also encouraged to export so they could acquire foreign exchange (US dollars, German marks) needed to buy products like machinery and oil, essential ingredients for industrialization. But this little plan soon backfired. Growing cash crops instead of food for local consumption led to increased reliance on food imports, which became relatively more expensive as commodity prices fell and local currencies lost value.

In short, the increase in interest rates coincided with falling commodity prices. Through no fault of its own, the Third World was suddenly faced with higher expenditures (in terms of increased debt maintenance) and lower income (due to falling commodity prices). Rather than going towards the purchase of products to modernize Third World economies as originally intended, foreign exchange went to pay foreign debts. It is important to keep in mind that these developments were not the result of the natural workings of the market but were initially orchestrated by the First World. In direct contradiction of free market doctrines, these programs were forced onto poor countries, illustrating once again that laissez-faire is planned. And badly planned at that.

Consequently, Third World debt soared, resulting in the 1980s debt crisis. At least from the perspective of the Third World, this crisis has yet to be resolved. Rather than take the blame and eliminate Third World debt, or at least substantially alleviate it, the World Bank used this opportunity to provide the Third World with another dose of First World medicine. When a country is in danger of defaulting on its debt, the

World Bank and the IMF step in with emergency measures. The logic behind these programs is that the only remedy that will work is strict adherence to free market principles. These programs, commonly referred to as austerity programs, are officially known as Structural Adjustment Programs (SAP). These include privatization and downsizing of government; the promotion of exports and liberalization of imports; reduction or even elimination of subsidies to agriculture, food, health care, and education; and programs to curb inflation (including higher interest rates and reduction in wages).[69]

Not surprisingly, these programs have failed to meet their objectives. Third World debt has continued to increase and its economies have faltered. The IMF and the World Bank have come under increasing scrutiny for their policies, both from the inside (including Joseph Stiglitz, the 2001 Nobel Prize winner in economics and former chief economist of the World Bank, who shared the prize with George Akerlof and Michael Spence) and the outside (the most prominent of their many critics being Paul David Hewson; a.k.a. the short guy with the funny glasses; a.k.a. Bono, the lead singer of the pop group U2).

The IMF (International Monetary Fund)

Like the World Bank, the IMF is part of the UN and a direct result of the Bretton Woods negotiations. The IMF, in particular, has been criticized for being overly secretive, and has historically been much less open to criticism than the World Bank. The IMF's major concern is international monetary cooperation and stability. When an emergency situation arises, such as balance of payment problems, currency instability, or inability to meet financial obligations, the IMF steps in and provides emergency loans. As of 2001, the IMF had approximately US $65 billion of loans outstanding. As with World Bank loans, monies are tied to SAPs, which gives the IMF considerable sway over how a country's economy is managed. In comparison with the World Bank, details of what the IMF does are less clear. This can partly be blamed on the already mentioned lack of transparency. The World Bank also has the advantage of sharing similarities with regular banks, in that it lends money, which is easy to understand. Besides having no domestic counterpart, the responsibilities of the IMF are a little more technical.[70] Furthermore, the IMF's mandate has changed considerably since its inception.

The primary role of the IMF following the Second World War was to supervise exchange rates. This was known as the Bretton Woods exchange system, whereby each country's currency was pegged to the American dollar, which, in turn, was pegged to the price of gold at US $35 per ounce. Some Canadians may remember that the price of foreign currencies, including that of the American dollar, fluctuated little between the war and the mid-1970s. For a variety of reasons, former US president Richard Nixon abandoned that system in 1971, and currencies were allowed to float. Suddenly, the price of currencies around the world became much more volatile (and as Canadians know too well, seemed only to drop). With the closing of the gold window, as it is sometimes referred to, one of the major responsibilities of the IMF had evaporated. But other commitments soon presented themselves. With the rapid rise in oil prices throughout the 1970s (which hurt importing countries) and the increase in interest rates (which hurt indebted countries), the IMF began to concentrate on short-term loans to countries that encountered balance of payment difficulties. Its role was further expanded when a series of Third World countries, starting with Mexico in 1982, came perilously close to defaulting on their debts.

The IMF also played a prominent role in the 1998 Asian crisis, but this debacle differed significantly from the 1980s debt crisis. The latter was largely caused by the increase in interest rates and affected mostly governments and big private banks. In contrast, in the Asian crisis the majority of investments were speculative in nature and involved private investors. Much of the foreign financing that had gone into Indonesia, South Korea, and Thailand went into risky ventures such as real estate speculation, and critics have pointed out that IMF loans did more for American, Japanese, and European investors than for the governments directly affected by the crisis. While the IMF guaranteed the investments of Westerners, austerity measures imposed on Indonesia, including the prohibition of subsidies for rice and cooking fuel, almost certainly contributed to the social unrest that the country underwent in 1999. According to the rules of the market, investors who greedily bankrolled foreign undertakings they knew little about should have suffered their own losses. But as it turned out, this was just another example of how institutions like the IMF are unable to stand by and do nothing when the judgment of the market fails to meet their expectations.

The Theory Behind Development

Essentially, the World Bank, the IMF, and the WTO are attempting to universalize the doctrines of laissez-faire, an ideology that, as we saw in previous chapters, originated in Great Britain in the eighteenth and nineteenth centuries. From there, mirroring colonization, it travelled to North America, Australia, and New Zealand, where the ideology still dominates. These ideas were also exported to other British colonies, including India and South Africa, and leaped the English Channel to the Continent, but there laissez-faire found a less welcoming environment and was tempered by the moderating influences of the host countries. In the twentieth century, dissemination of the free market ideology has continued unabated. It has now become the mission of institutions like the WTO and the World Bank to disseminate and enforce these ideas in the Third World.

Another important ideology that underlies institutions like the World Bank, the WTO, and the IMF is the old saw, promulgated by early social theorists, that societies must go through an evolution of stages on their way to industrial status. It is worthwhile noting that this thesis, usually referred to as modernization theory, has, in a variety of incarnations, been around for centuries, and yet its more optimistic prophecies have never come to fruition. This theory became fashionable in eighteenth- and nineteenth-century Europe, and attempted to explain the transition from an agricultural to an urban society. This change was accompanied by much tumult, and social theorists shared a desire to make sense of it all. Whereas some, like Adam Smith, saw order, others, like Karl Marx, saw chaos. Based on their observations, these theorists sought to establish principles from which they could generalize; that is, to apply their theories to all times and places. Not surprisingly, these theorists all observed a society that was slowly evolving from agrarian to industrial status. This evolutionary element provided an integral component for many theories, including those of French theorist Emile Durkheim, the Englishman Herbert Spencer, and the German Ferdinand Tönnies. All contrasted a decaying feudal, traditional, or agricultural order with a burgeoning industrial, urban, or modern one. Marx's theory stood apart only in that it had more stages—primitive communism, slavery, feudalism, capitalism, socialism, and communism—but the underlying evolutionary impetus was the same. Many academics have judged these theories as perspicacious for their time, but are reluctant to vouch for their universal application. This hesitancy is understandable for, given the benefit of hindsight, we know that not all societies have gone through these same stages of evolution. As a matter of fact, to this day there are still more people on this planet toiling away in agrarian than industrial societies.

The fact that theories of evolution have been discredited by more than two hundred years of history has not discouraged twentieth-century pundits from continuing with this train of thought. Today these theories comfortably fit under the rubric of modernization theory. Its proponents point to countries like Taiwan and South Korea as evidence of what is in store for the rest of the world. Beyond that, they forecast the eventual industrialization, and eventually post-industrialization, of all countries. In essence, these theories are no different than those espoused by theorists in the eighteenth century. The only difference is that today this thesis has left the theoretical realm and found practical applications through institutions like the World Bank and the WTO.

In Praise of Sweatshops

Suffering under the delusion that the West's economic success is rooted in laissez-faire, organizations like the WTO and the World Bank have put their faith in the market to solve the problem of global inequality. These institutions, as well as free traders in general, allege that open markets will eventually increase the wealth of all those who choose to participate in the global economy. Advocates of free trade have used this line of reasoning in a roundabout way to attack anti–free traders, accusing them of being anti-poor. They argue that by denying poor countries the opportunity to trade, anti-globalists also deny them a chance to become wealthy. But this road to wealth, we are forewarned, is a long one, and we cannot expect results to happen overnight. In a provocatively titled article, "In Praise of Sweatshops," Marcus Gee of *The Globe and Mail* argues that in order to benefit from the global economy, poor countries must start with workers toiling away in sweatshops making plastic flowers, but that soon they "move onto tennis rackets, then cellular phones, then automobile parts. Incomes rise and income inequalities drops."[71] Further, he argues that "Countries that shut themselves off from the global economy languish in poverty. Countries that join it prosper and grow" and that "an overwhelming body of evidence shows that globalization is the best antidote to poverty." The intent of the article is to show how wrongheaded anti-globalists are. "[Demonstrators] want to strip poor countries of their only competitive advantage—cheap labour. . . . But sweatshops are precisely what poor countries need. They are the first step to economic takeoff . . . that almost every successful country has had to take."

Although not explicit, the similarities between Gee's article and modernization theory are apparent. The gist of his little parable is that an economy needs to evolve from plastic flowers to automobile parts. Gee, in common with modernization theorists, has a tendency to universalize from selective examples. He points to exceptional cases like Japan and South Korea, yet ignores the one hundred or so other countries that continue to toil in poverty. As it turns out, the "overwhelming body of evidence" he refers to is not all that. Gee fails to include the results of even a single study and one can only guess what research he is referring to. Not surprisingly, the evidence that does exist reveals a trend that is exactly the opposite of what Gee would have us believe. In 1950, the GDP per capita of industrialized countries (excluding Japan) was approximately double that of Third World countries. By 1998, this gap had widened considerably, as the industrial countries' GDP per capita had increased to approximately five times that of the Third World. Whereas that of Asia and Latin America increased marginally (approximately doubling), GDP per capita failed to increase in Africa and dropped to 1950s levels after the fall of communism in the erstwhile Soviet countries.

And the further one goes back, the more apparent becomes the growing disparity in wealth between the First and Third worlds. Angus Maddison, an economic historian with the OECD (Organisation for Economic Co-operation and Development), has examined the incomes of six regions over a 172-year period (Western Europe, North America, and Australia make up one region; Eastern Europe, Southern Europe, Latin America, Asia, and Africa are the other five).[72] In 1820, the ratio of economic output between the richest and poorest of these regions was 3:1. From that date on, the world economy grew at a monumental rate, although this growth affected each region differently. This should not be unexpected, given colonization as well as huge gaps in technology. Trade throughout that period also increased, particularly in the post-war era. At any rate, between 1820 and 1992 the ratio between the richest and poorest regions had grown from the original 3:1 to 16:1. When countries are considered instead of regions, this disparity becomes even more dramatic, growing from 3:1 in 1820 to 72:1 in 1992. At no time throughout this period did this process of polarization let up, let alone reverse. This even applies to the very prosperous post-war era, a period throughout which trade increased dramatically. The World Bank, despite claims that globalization is supposed to provide opportunities for less-developed countries, has published similar data. In terms of wealth, then, the world was a much more egalitarian place in the 1820s than in the 1990s, casting a shadow of doubt on theories that project a better future for the Third World on the basis of free trade or industrialization. Such promises have failed to materialize in the past 180 years and there is no reason to believe that they will bear fruit any time soon.

These theories, as advocated by Gee, the World Bank, and the WTO, have failed to produce the predicted results because they ignore the interrelationships between countries, particularly that of the First and Third worlds. Sociologists are keenly aware of how power imbalances affect relationships, whether between individuals or groups. From that perspective, it becomes clear that not all countries are equal. Suriname cannot boast the same influence on the world stage as the United States, for example. The reason, as Andre Gunder Frank has pointed out, is a history of colonialism.

While that era has largely come to an end, First World countries continue to exert considerable power over the Third World in other, primarily economic, ways.

One reason that this disparity of wealth endures is precisely because of organizations like the World Bank and the WTO. Third World debt in 1998 was US $2.4 trillion (that's twelve zeros and approximately three and a half times Canada's yearly GDP). That same year, in order to service that debt, Third World countries paid US $296 billion in interest payments. This is more money than travelled the other direction in terms of aid. In other words, the industrialized world continues to be a net benefactor in this relationship. In the process, Third World economies are slowly being enslaved on account of their debts. For example, in Zambia 30 percent of government spending goes to paying off foreign debt, with only 10 percent going to social services, including health and education.

Ironically, despite their allegiance to free markets, these institutions are unable to keep their hands off them. First, they feel the inevitable evolutionary process towards modernization has to be nudged along, which does not necessarily have to be a bad thing. The transference of technology, knowledge, or capital investment can be of utmost value to poor countries. But even if modernization theory were correct in its fundamental premise that societies evolve, it does not necessarily follow that this process can be hurried along. There is good reason to believe that too quick a transition can ruin, rather than benefit, an economy. Witness, for example, the devastation that followed the sudden collapse of the Soviet economy a little over a decade ago. The transition from socialism to free market meant the economy went into free fall. When change is too rapid, or imposed from the outside as is often the case in the Third World, the effect may not always be that favourable. Second, the World Bank has always worked on the assumption that what is good for the First World must be equally good for the Third. But taken out of their Western context, free trade, privatization, and strict monetary policies have caused more ill to Third World economies than good. Not that free trade, privatization, and strict monetary policies have been all that successful in the First World either, but such policies make even less sense in economies that are still primarily agricultural.

And last, but not least, the evidence showing that First World countries are wealthy because of their strict adherence to free market principles is far from conclusive. First, the benefits of free trade, as we have discussed, are dubious to begin with. Second, First World countries all have generous education and health programs, which they sometimes deny to Third World countries. (Even in the United States, often considered a welfare-state laggard, 45 percent of health care is publicly funded, which amounted to US $522 billion in 1998. Publicly funded education cost another US $498 billion in the 1998–1999 school year, which adds up to over $1 trillion in government expenditures on a yearly basis for these two programs alone.) Industrialized countries also have huge civil services that provide many well-paying jobs. Third, there is consideration neither of differences in culture, nor of the power relationship, between the First and Third worlds. When intervention is neutral (that is, money comes with no strings attached), it may not be altogether bad. But as we have seen, in its eagerness to pull the Third World out of poverty,

First World policies have only succeeded in making the Third World go into more debt.

This is not to say that debt should be avoided at all costs. In order for economies to grow, they require capital, and borrowing funds can play an invaluable role in this process. The expansion of the British Empire was expedited by the availability of easy money, and many governments today borrow money to invest in their future. But there is a crucial difference between First and Third world debt, in that the former is usually owed internally and the latter externally. The biggest shortcoming associated with foreign debt is the control that the lender is able to exert over the indebted. It is precisely for this reason that many religions have proscribed debt. The Bible counsels that "the borrower is a servant to the lender." In that sense, large debts have enslaved Third World countries, making it difficult for them to become independent. Programs that have attempted to alleviate debts through rescheduling, such as the notorious SAP, have only succeeded in imposing more Western control over the Third World.

The Power Dynamics of Trade

As we just saw, poor countries are trading more, yet they continue to be poor, and are even getting poorer, at least relatively speaking, in the process. One reason for this widening gap may be that not all trade is necessarily fair. Adam Smith conjectured that there was a natural price level related to the hours of labour needed to produce an item. He wrote "[if it takes] twice the labour to kill a beaver which it does to kill a deer, one beaver should naturally exchange for or be worth two deer."[73] This might work well in theory, but fails in practice because it does not acknowledge differences in knowledge, education, and power. A lawyer is in a much better position to boss her secretary around than vice versa. Similarly, rich industrial countries are better able to dictate the terms of trade than their poorer counterparts. Third World countries, with huge numbers of unemployed and few options, are seldom in a favourable position to negotiate a fair deal. The fact that poor countries have not been able to gain access to the food and textile markets, the areas they are best able to compete in, well illustrates the point. In addition, when organizations like the World Bank and the IMF insist that debts must be paid off, countries feel coerced into making deals that they might have turned down otherwise.

Poor countries also have to deal with pressures that so-called mature economies do not face. As previously mentioned, the majority of Third World debts are foreign, which usually translates into a litany of demands by the World Bank and the IMF. In addition, the currencies of poor countries are not widely accepted (usually referred to as soft currencies) and they require hard currencies (the US dollar and euro) to buy essentials like oil or pay off debts. In contrast, Western countries are free from these constraints: They do not have to answer to institutions like the World Bank and usually need not worry about having their currencies accepted abroad. This puts poor countries in a vulnerable position, and most are desperate to sell what they have at any price. Since there are so many poor countries competing against one another, the rich countries have been able to play them off one another and shop for the best deal.

Power can also explain why not all endowments and skills are rewarded equally. Why does coffee cost so little and pharmaceutical products and oil so much? One reason is that oil producers and pharmaceutical companies have been able to control prices through cartelization and patent protection. Coffee producers have not been able to organize to the same effect (although they have tried). In turn, Third World countries are unable to afford products from the West because of patent protection, which essentially allows for protected monopolies. Whoever is able to get together and fix prices, secure patent protection, or gain other such favours from governments or the WTO is in a much better position to profit from the world economy. Largely, this is determined by who has the financial, and intricately related, legal resources to influence those institutions. For this and a host of other reasons, Third World countries are less than enthusiastic about free trade, as they feel their needs are not adequately addressed. All of the items currently on the agenda of the WTO—from intellectual property rights and foreign investment protection to trades in services—have been lobbied for by the First World and are unlikely to benefit the Third. As a matter of fact, these regulations are likely to result in higher prices for high-tech products in poor countries, thus making them worse off. Because of patent protection, drug prices are out of reach for most people in the Third World and they become sicker and even die. No one has summarized the absurdity of this situation better than Joseph Stiglitz, who commented in a interview that "we don't care if people die, intellectual property rights are really supreme."[74]

Agriculture and Textiles

One of the most persistent stumbling blocks on the road to free trade has been agriculture. It is also the issue that most divides the First and the Third worlds. At an average of 40 percent on a global basis, compared with single-digit levels for manufactured goods, tariffs for agricultural products continue to be high. Even more damaging than tariffs are the huge subsidies that wealthy countries use to prop up their agricultural industries. In the absence of such subsidies, agriculture would not be able to survive in most high-wage economies, thus taking away business from low-wage countries.

Agriculture is one of the few industries that poor countries are able to compete in, and the continuation of generous subsidies for agriculture in the West suggests a First World bias in the WTO. The alternative of waging a subsidy war is just not an option for the Third World, as the dollar figures are prohibitively high. Most guilty of this kind of protectionism is the EU and its Common Agricultural Policy (CAP). France is probably the most stubborn defender of subsidies, with Japan following not far behind. The United States and Canada, even Mexico, also engage in subsidies, although to a lesser extent. (They do so, they say, in order to compete with Europe and Japan.) In 1998, agricultural subsidies amounted to US $360 billion in the OECD world.[75] This number may not mean much on its own, but it is shockingly high given that world trade in agricultural products that same year was only US $456. In Japan, subsidies amount to over 60 percent of all farm receipts. In the EU, they exceed 40 percent. In the United States and Canada, this figure hovers around the 20 percent mark, slightly lower but still high enough to make it impossible for the Third World to compete.[76] Canada has also been successful in keeping the Canadian Wheat Board in place, which contributes to artificially high prices. To be fair, the WTO has rebuked Western countries, including Canada, for keeping import quotas on agricultural products, but this has been to no avail. This may be just another indication of the impotence of the organization, and shows how free trade, particularly for the Third World, is anything but.

Why have rich countries been so reluctant to dismantle their barriers to free trade in agriculture? On the surface, this behaviour makes little sense, as agriculture constitutes such an insignificant portion of First World economies. In Canada, for example, agriculture employs fewer than 2 percent of the population and amounts to even less in terms of GDP. The reasons are obviously not financial then. Instead, they are all about self-sufficiency and security. All of the following reasons are also part of CAP, the most ardent defender of agricultural subsidies. Europe and Japan are reluctant to abolish agricultural subsidies because they fear that this could result in a series of unpleasant scenarios. First, and probably the most important, is that in times of war a country not self-sufficient in food would be an easy target for military takeover. Japan and Europe, for example, where memories of the Second World War still linger, are understandably unwilling to take that risk. The WTO usually claims that trading nations do not go to war, but if this were really such a remote possibility, why not abolish military subsidies? Second, governments are justifiably concerned about food safety. In case of a worldwide drought or disease, countries do not want to find themselves in the precarious situation of being wholly dependent on imports. Third, and related to the previous point, shortages of food elsewhere can mean higher prices at home. In the Third World, where increasingly more farmers are switching to cash crops, dependence on food imports has already resulted in more costly food. With domestic production, such shocks can be mitigated to at least some degree. Even without natural shortages, a country could monopolize a segment of the industry and then charge prices accordingly. A fourth defence, used by France, is that by subsidizing agriculture, it is preserving a way of life.

Defenders of free trade usually oppose subsidies because they inevitably translate into higher prices for the consumer. Without such subsidies, the OECD has calculated, prices for food would be about one-third lower.[77] But given the concerns just enumerated, consumers would likely consent to paying that little extra for what could be considered a security premium. Even if consumers do prefer to pay less, one could argue that it is a government's responsibility to ensure that such a crisis is, if at all possible, averted. Say France abandoned its wheat industry by discontinuing subsidies, thereby having to depend on imports. Suppose further that the entire North American wheat crop was devastated by a drought. Prices for wheat around the world would soon skyrocket and importing countries would be faced with the unenviable dilemma of choosing between exorbitant prices or curtailing consumption. Who would the citizenry blame? The weather, foreign farmers, or their governments for failing to have the foresight to anticipate such an event?

The problem of agriculture continues to dog the WTO, and there appears to be no practicable solution in sight. Laws protecting agriculture go back to at least the 1400s, and, as we saw, were central to the fight over free trade in nineteenth-century Great Britain. Over a century and a half later, the issue of agricultural subsidies has yet to be resolved. If subsidies prevail, there will certainly be no justice for the Third World.

On the other hand, an imposed solution, wherein First World countries are forced to give up subsidies and subsequently risk losing their agricultural industries—all in the name of free trade—seems neither fair nor sensible.

Third World countries find it difficult to compete with the First World primarily because of their lack of technology and trained workforce. The exception to this is the clothing and textiles industry. Besides agriculture, it is one of the few industries in which the Third World can compete on an equal footing, mostly because the industry does not require sophisticated technology. Most production in the Third World still takes place within the household, including the production and mending of clothes. As a result, most women in the Third World know how to sew. Foreign and domestic firms have been quick to exploit these skills, and as many people are aware, a large share of clothes purchased in the First World are currently imported from the Third. The most important of these producers is Asia. Because of the Third World's competitive edge in this field, First World countries have been reluctant to remove trade barriers. Canada's tariffs for clothing and textiles are 16.6 and 11.7 percent respectively, with figures for the United States and Europe only slightly lower. These are only the most explicit barriers, and many First World countries also actively engage in non-tariff barriers like quotas. In contrast to agriculture, reasons for these barriers are nothing less than old-fashioned protectionism. The fact is that Canada, the United States, and Europe simply want to preserve their struggling clothing industries and they know that without protection these would be destined for extinction.

Agriculture and textiles highlight some of the difficulties associated with free trade. On the one hand, it is easy to understand why countries want to protect these industries. This is most apparent with respect to food. On the other hand, by not liberalizing these markets and denying the Third World a fair chance to compete, free trade amounts to little more than a farce. The Third World ends up paying higher prices for products from the West as a result of patent protection and the monopolization of technology, yet is held back from freely competing in the two industries in which it could profit: agriculture and textiles.

The Road to Riches

Most economists working throughout the Depression insisted that, based on the model of supply and demand, workers should accept low wages because of a weak demand for labour. They also maintained that low wages were only a temporary setback, and predicted that as the economy improved, demand for workers would increase, as would wages. But according to John Maynard Keynes, a return to high employment was going to take such a long time that most workers were unlikely to see the day. On this basis, he urged governments to intervene. There is an obvious corollary to be made here between the Depression and the current situation in the Third World. To paraphrase Keynes, by the time poor countries are able to benefit from free trade we will be all dead, and then some. In the Third World, there is no reason for workers' wages to rise, as there is no shortage of workers in the foreseeable, or even far, future. Unlike in Adam Smith's time, the supply of labour no longer fluctuates with wages. And similar to during the Depression, the supply of workers in the Third World is so vast that it is unlikely there will ever be more work than workers, the only situation in which workers can credibly make wage demands. Furthermore, again as in the Depression, low wages in the Third World mean workers have little money to spend on consumer products, such consumption being so important to the growth of an economy.

As we have seen, it is commonly believed that poor countries will spend only a limited time in the low-wage sector, after which they will evolve into industrial economies and beyond. But this evolution is frustrated by the fact that most markets are already saturated. First World corporations already have such a stranglehold on existing markets that it becomes exceedingly challenging for new companies to penetrate them. This is particularly true for poor countries. To start manufacturing cars, for example, is a business venture likely to end in failure, as there are already far too many firms competing. Particularly without the help of subsidies, strictly prohibited by the WTO, new entrants are doomed to failure. Countries wishing to industrialize are destined to hit roadblocks never encountered by countries like Great Britain and the United States. When these countries first industrialized they faced little competition; at the same time, profligate subsidies and other forms of protectionism were a matter of course. In that sense, the race for the global economy started centuries ago, and it is only now, when the First World is already over the finish line, that the Third World has been invited to compete.

Economists are reluctant to acknowledge such power imbalances. Often overlooked as well is the fact that the rich countries are able to use their economic clout to assist, rather than hinder, the development of poor countries. After the Second World War, the United States, realizing that a bankrupt Europe (and Germany in particular) would likely remain economically devastated, introduced the Marshall Plan, which gave (not lent) these countries US $13 billion so they could rebuild their economies. While it is true that the Marshall Plan was partly motivated by the fear that Europe might turn communist, this does not take away from the fact that these substantial infusions of cash allowed Germany and other European countries to regain their economic momentum. Parallel developments occurred under the supervision of General Douglas MacArthur, who oversaw the social, political, and economic reconstruction of Japan after the Second World War. Obviously, these programs worked, as Japan and Germany are now the second and third most powerful economies in the world. Similarly, in the EU, billions of dollars have been transferred from the rich northern countries (Germany, France) to the poorer southern ones (Spain, Greece). The European Commission realized that its less well-off members would not be able to compete on a level playing field without subsidies. The costs of these programs ran into the billions of dollars, yet the European economy has not collapsed. The West could surely implement similar programs without too much hardship. Such details are too often forgotten, but must be remembered if the Third World is going to have any chance of joining the world economy.

Conclusion

The West must closely examine its policies vis-à-vis the Third World, admit they have failed, and restrategize. To state the obvious, if something has not worked in fifty years it is time either to fix it or throw it out. If the First World is indeed serious about Third World poverty, it must do more than simply provide loans and offer platitudes about the superiority of the market. First of all, the First World must take some responsibility for the debt crisis that has afflicted the Third World for over two decades now, and either forgive or drastically reduce these loans. The First World must also generously share its technology, rather than hoard it with legislation that protects intellectual property and patents. Having to pay a high premium for technology—drugs, computers, machinery, disease-resistant seeds—will only widen the chasm between rich and poor. Even if technology were shared freely, it would take decades before the workforce in poor countries was educated enough to harness its benefits.

9

PRODUCTION, CONSUMPTION, AND EMPLOYMENT: WILL THE CIRCLE BE UNBROKEN?

I N AN EDITORIAL ABOUT FREE TRADE, *The Globe and Mail* was unable to make sense of the inconsistency between President Bush's speech and his actions.[78] On the one hand, he trotted out shibboleths like, "When we negotiate for open markets, we are providing new hope for the world's poor" and "when we promote free trade, we are promoting political freedom." On the other hand, Bush was simultaneously supporting investigations that were destined to result in tariffs against imports of softwood lumber, steel, and wheat. Many people are puzzled by such contradictory, nonetheless pervasive, behaviour. This chapter is going to examine more closely this

194

apparent contradiction and show that Bush's behaviour is not all that difficult to understand and is, in fact, economically speaking, quite rational.

The reason Bush acts the way he does is that the WTO puts governments in an awkward position. It asks everybody to keep the faith and promises an often-nervous public that once all countries focus on their strengths and resist engaging in protectionism, all countries will be better off. This prisoner's dilemma for governments may work fine in theory, but given there is little evidence that free trade policies bring about anything other than more free trade, it is easy to appreciate that few are willing to take this leap from the theoretical to the practical. And until some concrete evidence is presented that shows free trade is of benefit even to those who do not engage in protectionism, governments will continue to be reluctant to keep their hands off the market. To put it another way, if free trade really did benefit everybody, countries would surely have figured this out by now. As the relationship between education and income illustrates, people are quick to learn when something does work. Even as it becomes more difficult to attend university, due to higher entrance requirements and increased tuition fees, people still want to go. On the other hand, people are significantly less enthusiastic about free trade and often do everything in their power to shelter themselves from the free market. This should tell us something about how people really feel.

The free trade theory fails because it accentuates the positive while completely ignoring the downside of open borders. This is similar to functionalism, a theory of society popular in the 1950s and 1960s, which judged the gender division of labour in the family as beneficial to all of society. Women raised children and worked in the home, and men toiled away in factories and offices and brought in money. But feminists pointed out that while this arrangement was a great advantage for men, it generally ignored the interests of half the population, women. Fifty years later, primarily because of the women's movement, we now realize that the division of labour in the family is neither natural nor fair. The theory of free trade is similar in that it chooses to ignore completely the segment of the population that does not benefit from open borders. In the real world, however, such interests are less easily ignored. Consequently, politicians like Bush feel pressured to act in ways that are inconsistent with the theory of free trade. But taken out of the theoretical realm, Bush's behaviour is easy to understand. The risks associated with doing nothing make it politically and economically just not worth keeping the faith.

Free trade is not, as they are so fond of saying in business, a "win-win" situation. If that were the case, everybody would be only too happy to sit back and enjoy its rewards. Rather, in the majority of instances, there are easily identifiable winners and losers. Moreover, people are quite capable of assessing on which side of the equation their interests fall and act accordingly. Countries that support free trade can be loosely summarized as those with strong export industries. In contrast, countries that are less competitive are less enthusiastic about open borders. Canada and the United States fall clearly in the former category, as both are technologically advanced and competitive in many industries, particularly the ascending knowledge industries of the "new economy" (hence the push to trade services). Canada also has more resources than it can consume and heavily relies on foreign markets for its "old economy" products. But this does not automatically mean that everybody in Canada supports open borders. Opposition naturally exists among industries that anticipate being injured by free trade. News stories about trade disputes are a testament to these clashing interests. To give but a couple of recent examples, American producers of softwood lumber seek protection from the more competitive Canadian industry. At the same time, Canadian dairy producers support policies that keep American ones outside their market.

Consequently, material interests are a much better predictor of who is likely to support free trade than is government policy or ideology. Thus we find time and again that politicians or industries that support free trade are quick to abandon it once it fails to work in their favour. Such ideological flip-flops are equally common when the situation is reversed. In a competitive position, even the most unlikely candidates support open borders. Bob Rae, past premier of Ontario and an outspoken critic of free trade during the negotiations with the United States in the late 1980s, was appointed to study the softwood dispute in 2001. To read some of his proclamations on the topic, one could easily get the impression that Rae had become a disciple of David Ricardo. But this is hardly the case, for Rae was simply defending a position where Canada would do well by free trade. Another example illustrative of this seeming contradiction is Oxfam. Oxfam, a well-known charity organization that fights poverty in the Third World, also conducts extensive research on economic issues. On its Web page, it proudly declares its official position is against free trade. At the same time, it highlights a study it commissioned that argues for free trade in textiles. The study claims, and correctly so, that free trade in these products would benefit many poor countries. Again, an example of an unlikely candidate promoting free trade when convenient.

Now free traders demand that people take a consistent position. They feel that if someone argues for free trade in one instance, he should want free trade for everything and at all times. In this, the right has been successful in forcing the range of opinion into one of two options: for or against. Within this framework, there is little room for a middle ground, for an "it depends" or "sometimes" answer, which is better suited to most real-world problems. Given this limited choice, countries are forced to adopt either one or the other position. This is true for industries as well. Thus an industry or country may support free trade only because it sees its immediate interests tied to that position. But free traders confuse that self-interest with genuine support for free trade in general. Based on rather skimpy evidence, free traders have been successful in convincing themselves, as well as some powerful politicians, that those who promote free trade are more noble, brave, and far-seeing than those who protect their industries. In fact, industries only use the free trade argument when it is convenient and serves their material interest. Although this self-interest is understandable in the context of a society that celebrates such sentiments, there is little that is noble about it.

As we have seen, Adam Smith thought self-interest should be encouraged on the basis that it served the common good. Yet self-interest can go both ways, as it can compel industries, depending on their level of competitiveness, to lobby either for open or closed borders. In the 1940s, when the US steel industry reigned supreme, it lobbied for free trade. Now that it has to compete with South Korea and Japan, it lobbies to have its markets protected. As this example illustrates, people tend to act on the basis of self-interest and not according to some abstract theory. Often industries support free trade for no other reason than it will allow them access to foreign markets, and they oppose it when they are likely to suffer from foreign competition. Free traders, who encourage self-interest as the foundation for open markets, need to understand that people are also acting in their self-interest when they seek to protect their jobs. Self-interest is not a switch that can conveniently be turned on or off depending on the health of one's industry.

If interests obviously diverge when it comes to free trade, why does there appear such uniformity of opinion on the issue among governments and the mainstream media? The most obvious answer to this is the power of ideology. Not surprisingly, those least likely to be affected by open borders are also its most vocal and consistent promoters: journalists, politicians, and academics. These groups have the luxury of working in a theoretical vacuum, their jobs being safely removed from the vagaries of the market. Most people working in the private sector are likely to be affected by free trade at some point in their lives. It is not too much of a stretch to assume that these people will change their opinion about free trade depending on how it affects their livelihood. And so it goes. People, organizations, whole countries champion free trade in industries in which they are competitive and clamour for protection in those in which they are weak. To strip the argument to its core, governments want jobs for their constituents and sometimes free trade may be the quickest route to that objective. At other times, protectionism is a more effective way of reaching that goal. Strong export industries mean jobs, but so do well-protected domestic industries.

Of course, the greatest number of jobs is gained if a country selectively does both, as all countries have been known to do at one time or another.

Production: The Other Side of the Coin

Central to the argument for free trade are the benefits that are supposed to accrue to the consumer. When critics rail against tariffs and protected markets, they justify their claim on the basis that it ultimately costs more for the consumer. Like much of the free trade argument, this one also owes a debt to Adam Smith. Smith argued that no organization, and in particular no government, could adequately assess what the consumer wanted. Any decisions made by committee were likely to be misguided and end in failure. The emphasis on the consumer has meant that the producer has become all but forgotten. As Smith originally wrote: "The interest of the producer ought to be attended to only so far as it may be necessary for promoting that of the consumer."[79] This position continues to find resonance today, and any policy designed to protect producers through either tariffs or subsidies is scorned.

Some economists have taken the consumer-is-king position to its logical conclusion and contended that, as an example, the United States should be happy to abandon its automobile industry to the Japanese, as in the end this would give the American consumer cheaper and better cars. According to this line of logic, the United States could then concentrate its energies on something it is good at, like building airplanes, designing computer software, or entertaining the world (or putting people in jail, but that service does not trade very well). Now I enjoy a good bargain myself and fully support consumer benefits, but realize that I am also a producer. This equation is painfully clear to me: If I do not produce, I do not consume, or at least not much beyond a subsistence level. And what is true for an individual is also true for a country.

This brings us to what is, at least in my opinion, the biggest shortcoming of the free trade thesis: It completely and sometimes wilfully ignores production. We should remember that the word "economy" is derived from the Greek word meaning household and there are obvious parallels to be drawn between its historical and contemporary meanings. If no one in a household works, its members will not be able to purchase goods or services no matter how low prices go. The same is true in an economy; if no one produces, no one consumes. The centrality of production is apparent in the way economies are measured. Economic success is measured by production, not consumption. A robust economy means higher economic output (GDP), not cheaper consumer products. In a booming economy, prices are often higher whereas prices in a recession are lower. This might be good for the consumer, but only a few would argue that a recession is a good thing based on that logic.[80]

The importance of production can be further demonstrated via a simple pop quiz. Which province would the reader relocate to if she were looking for work, Newfoundland or Alberta? People intuitively know that production is important and move to where the jobs are and not where consumer products are cheapest. World migration patterns have followed that simple logic for centuries. The same is true within Canada: People move to where the jobs are. Many products, such as housing, are cheaper in Newfoundland (good for the consumer), but that means little without the production end providing jobs. Recently, the township of Tumbler Ridge, a dying coal-mining town in northern British Columbia, auctioned off standard three-bedroom homes for around $10,000. Again, good for the consumer, but of little use without a job. One can similarly buy products cheaply anywhere in the Third World, say Vietnam, but few Canadians move there, as the production side of the equation is wanting. As a matter of fact, Canadians are much more likely to move to the United States where living expenses are even higher than in Canada—not a wise consumer decision, that—but there are plenty of well-paying jobs. On the other hand, when there are plenty of jobs, there are also affluent consumers. Ontario is now close to passing Michigan as the number one jurisdiction for production of automobiles, mini-vans, and small trucks in North America. It is also, by the way, one of the richest consumer markets in the world. The two go hand in hand. No production, no jobs, no consumers, no matter how far prices fall.

And therein lies the contradiction of free trade: Cheaper products mean lower wages, which will eventually work their way through the economy and affect everybody's standard of living. Most, if not all, governments behave in a way that reveals that they are aware of that contradiction, although most are reluctant to admit it. While the WTO counsels its members to follow the rules, few countries, including the most ardent supporters of free trade, are capable of abiding by those regulations once their economies are under threat.

As an interesting aside, even free traders do at times support production. This is revealed by their attitudes towards the Auto Pact. This agreement, signed between Canada and

the United States in 1964, is note *..*rthy because it is
consistently trotted out as a model of how trade can work to
the benefit of everybody. Interestingly, this support spans the
political spectrum. The left sees the pact as an exemplar of
managed trade, the right of free trade. Gordon Ritchie praises
the Auto Pact, which he calls the "single most successful
sectoral trade deal ever negotiated" that brought "extra-
ordinary benefits" to Canada for the next twenty-five years
after it was signed.[81] This is not to pick on Mr. Ritchie, but
his position reveals the unintentional self-deception that
free traders undergo when they are faced with success. His
faith in the market is blind to the fact that the Auto Pact
actually contravenes two very important free trade principles,
both of which are prohibited by the WTO: preferential
treatment and performance demands. First, the Auto Pact
discriminates against Japanese and European automakers, a
complaint that has already been taken to the WTO, which
decided against the United States and Canada. Second, the
Auto Pact requires that American manufacturers produce
as many cars in Canada as are sold. This is explicitly illegal
under the GATT, which prohibits any kinds of performance requirements attached to Foreign Direct Investment
(FDI). I do, however, agree with Mr. Ritchie that the Auto
Pact was a success and that we should negotiate more deals
like it. But the Auto Pact was only as successful as it was
because it focused on production, thereby guaranteeing
jobs for Canadian workers. As already said, the WTO has
dispensed with such preferences thereby making the most
"successful sectoral trade deal ever negotiated" impossible
to replicate.

Government

Much of free trade ideology is deeply rooted in a strong antipathy towards the state. Now there are any number of reasons why governments do and sometimes, dare I say, must, interfere in the economy, all of which focus on production rather than consumption. The following should not be interpreted as an argument for protectionism, but rather as an explanation for why governments around the world are so keen to maintain or assist their industries.[82] One argument against abandoning uncompetitive industries is that it takes time to establish new ones. We know from experience that once an industry disappears, job losses are immediate and enduring. It may take decades before a jurisdiction (city, province, country) is able to establish a new industry that replaces an old one, particularly one that provides a significant number of jobs. Sometimes it never happens. Even a cursory overview of North America shows that few have done so successfully. While Pittsburgh has replaced its dying steel industry with the high-tech sector, there are dozens of Newfoundlands that have failed to reclaim jobs lost. The gradual decline of the lumber industry in British Columbia has gone on for decades, yet there are few communities in rural British Columbia that have successfully adopted another industry.

Furthermore, what works for Pittsburgh cannot work for every jurisdiction. Given that North America is highly competitive in the high-tech sector, it is a popular industry for jurisdictions to pursue. Every armchair economist urges that her local or national government should establish its own high-tech sector. True, this industry does provide jobs that are well-paying, it is clean, and it can be quite profitable. At the same time, there are only a limited number of jobs available in this field, particularly after the crash the industry experienced in 2000. It is also difficult for new industries to compete with already established jurisdictions, such as Silicon Valley, Kanata, Boston, or Pittsburgh, to name just a few (made even more difficult by the fact that the industry is heavily subsidized by the military in the United States). Consequently, high-tech jobs are slow to replace jobs lost in the fishing or forest industries.

Despite the disappearance of whole industries, many people continue to live in economically depressed areas because of government programs such as employment insurance or subsidies to industries. Some economists would argue that these subsidies unnecessarily fetter technological progress. But even if income maintenance programs were abolished, it is hardly plausible that all of Canada's unemployed would migrate to Canada's urban centres. What would they do? Retrain? And for what? First, it takes time to retrain, from a minimum of six months for a diploma to four years for a university degree (which, by the way, also requires government funding). Even with university training, good jobs are becoming increasingly scarce and more education, such as a graduate degree, is required. As important, job openings are likely to be filled by young graduates rather than ex-loggers or fishers in their forties and fifties. In theory, it might be fine to let industries die a timely death, but practically, it would unfold as a logistical nightmare as hundreds of thousands of people would chase a limited number of jobs.

A second argument against letting industries fail is that there are few markets left to exploit. The fact of the matter is that the West can easily produce more goods and services than its citizens can possibly hope to consume. The Great Depression was caused by too many goods chasing too few consumers, and the situation is similar today: Markets everywhere are saturated. In such a competitive environment few governments are willing to let proven industries die, and understandably so. Furthermore, any new markets a country pursues are just as likely to be saturated as the old ones. Any number of countries is, roughly speaking, equally efficient at producing automobiles, steel, or airplanes, and a competitive advantage means little in these circumstances. Furthermore, whatever industry one may choose to compete in, there are only so many computers, automobiles, fridges, or video cameras that the public can buy. The risk of finding new markets is just too high and any country that allowed its present markets to be serviced by foreign competitors would surely do so at its own peril.

Now the counter-argument to intervention is, as economists are quick to point out, that it is difficult for governments to choose winners. Following, it is best to forbid them to interfere altogether. Again, this seems to be a legitimate criticism, but there are a number of problems with this observation. First, not all government intervention is alike. There is a big difference between the government directly operating a company, providing loan guarantees, or funding research. Second, all industrial countries—including the United States, Great Britain, Japan, and Canada—have sheltered their fledgling industries at one time or another with protective industrial policies. Why should this matter? Its seems just a little hypocritical for First World countries, having greatly benefited from protectionist policies in the past, to now dictate to emerging economies that they cannot make use of the same. Third, just because it is difficult to pick winners should not automatically exclude governments from the process. If such a policy were always adhered to, and no one took risks, capitalism itself would not exist. No risk, no stock market, no investment, no progress. It is difficult to pick winners at any level—careers, real estate, prime ministers—and to avoid a situation simply because it may end in failure would result in a country full of losers. As we saw in previous chapters, government has played a central role in the development of the Canadian economy, and few would deny that this intervention has been effective.

One need not point out that private institutions are no better at making decisions than are governments. Banks are notorious for making bad loans and overextending themselves. The failures of the Canadian Commercial Bank and Northland Bank in the 1980s are just two examples of this. Furthermore, the federal government stepped in and guaranteed that all deposits would be honoured. The American government acted similarly in the savings and loan scandal in the 1980s. In this respect, intervention is indispensable and governments needs to act as an insurer of last resort. Once a financial or physical disaster occurs and an insurance company or bank fails, a hands-off approach is likely to only worsen the situation. The actions of the American government following the September 11 terrorist attacks well illustrate the point. Should President Bush have just let the airlines perish? He did not, but immediately came to assist the industry with a quick infusion of cash (US $5 billion). Some foreign airlines were upset and complained about what they rightfully considered to be a subsidy, but given the alternative—a series of airline failures costing in the hundreds of billions of dollars—it was the right choice. This should make it quite apparent why various jurisdictions—be they countries, provinces, or municipalities—are loath to leave things to the market. Many politicians recognize that production is crucial to the economy and are willing to do whatever it takes to protect local industries, including using subsidies and tariffs. Free trade theory aside, both politicians and voters are acutely aware that once there are no jobs, there will soon be few consumers.

The approach advocated by free traders—that the dismantling of trade barriers benefits all—fails for two reasons. One, workers get upset when their jobs are threatened with extinction and are not likely to take such developments with equanimity. In the real world of politics, nostrums about the advantages of free trade are woefully inadequate and fall far short of appeasing those in danger of losing their livelihood. It is therefore in a politician's best interest (here we have that self-interest again) to do more for her constituents, and since politicians want to stay elected, they usually do end up responding to these demands. Political expediency also explains the contradictory attitudes of the United States. On the one hand, it is the number one advocate of free trade; on the other, it is quick to resort to protectionism. To some degree this is true for every country, for to sacrifice jobs in the name of free trade may sound good in theory, but it falls far short of guaranteeing success in the next election. Nor does it guarantee economic growth. In any case, there is so much interference in the economy already that to talk about free trade borders on hypocrisy.

Second, and as important, even on a level playing field countries are still not equal. Wealthier countries are much better positioned, both economically and technologically, to dominate any number of sectors in the economy. The West could easily dominate the world economy (as it already does to some degree). Less technologically sophisticated countries would be most disadvantaged, particularly as economies become more knowledge oriented. This explains why countries are reluctant to unconditionally accept the tenets of free trade. In practice, no country has ever been able to industrialize without at least some planning and protectionism. In this respect, trade agreements are laden with unrealistic expectations and have proven far too rigid to work effectively. While protectionist tactics may at times be counterproductive, it does not follow that this is always the case.

Conclusion

According to the rules of free trade, countries agree that if no one applies tariffs or uses subsidies, all will be better off. In contrast, self-interest prevails and participants abide by the rules only when it benefits them, the real objective for governments being national rather than international wealth. The participants in world trade are workers and industries who more than anything are interested in their own well-being, and they will quickly abandon the rules of free trade once they fail to work in their favour. Since the 1980s, the American pharmaceutical industry has been busy lobbying governments for open markets around the world. Is this because of self-interest or because of a firm belief in the tenets of free trade? Suppose that in future Asian drug companies develop better and cheaper drugs than the Americans. It would not be long before American pharmaceutical companies insisted that there was a need to protect local markets, all, of course, in the interest of national health. Such turncoat tactics, rather than being an anomaly, are actually closer to the way that international trade is currently conducted.

This chapter began by referring to an editorial that expressed surprise at the inconsistent behaviour that President Bush exhibited towards free trade. But Bush is only proclaiming to play the game of international free trade, whereas in fact he is playing the game of increasing domestic wealth. Free trade may help some jobs, in which case Bush is all too eager to support it. However, not all industries can benefit from free trade, and those that do not require different tactics, including tariffs and subsidies. Bush has to answer to a variety of interests, some of which want free trade and some that do not, and by covering all bases he hopes to make everybody happy. Most countries are aware of this ruse; few are willing to admit it. All Bush did was tell the truth.

A conclusion is the place where you got tired thinking.
—MARTIN H. FISHER

CONCLUSION:
THE FUTURE OF FREE TRADE

As ALREADY SAID, there is little doubt that trade brings with it certain benefits. However, from this it does not necessarily follow that more trade is always better. In other words, just because a little of something is good is no guarantee that more of the same is correspondingly better. There are many instances, salt, for example, where small amounts are essential, but larger quantities have precisely the opposite effect and may actually cause harm. The obvious moral to be drawn from this is that more is not always better. But this is exactly how the idea of free trade has been sold to us, the more the better. Yet these benefits are, as we have seen, illusory.

Despite questionable outcomes for economies around the world, commentators continue to pontificate about the blessings of free trade. Politicians, trade bureaucrats, and journalists lecture on its benefits, hoping their stance will make them appear well informed and full of conviction. In reality, though, it makes them look stale and unimaginative—we've heard it all before. In this day and age, an era when we are allegedly undergoing an information revolution, one should expect that we would have transcended the Big Idea stage of politics. And there is little doubt that there exists an appetite for a more informed debate on the topic of free trade but, alas, that has not been the case.

In light of all this, how is it that the topic of free trade has dominated the Canadian political and economic agenda for over a decade and a half? One reason is that politicians and the media prefer a simple Big Idea over a complicated one. Unfortunately, this is not the first time that a simple idea has come to dominate a political agenda. History is full of Big Ideas: Christianity is good, socialism is bad, capitalism is good, the deficit is bad. In one sense, we can consider ourselves fortunate in that the current obsession with free trade is relatively innocuous and rarely accompanied by violence. Nonetheless, that by no means makes it a more sophisticated or better idea.

Free trade, like any Big Idea, is appealing because it provides a simple, even simplistic, prescription for a series of complex problems. In Canada, it has provided a simple solution for many of the domestic and international problems that the country faces today. Whether the problem is a slowing economy, world hunger, or lagging productivity, the ready answer is always free trade. If such a panacea were to exist, it would truly be a wonderful thing. But the world is a complex place and does not lend itself to such facile solutions. The only result that more free trade agreements are likely to bring about is, well, more trade. And in the larger scheme of things, that just does not suffice.

As the evidence mounts against it, will free trade prove to be a spent force? The answer to this must be a resounding no; at least not for the foreseeable future. The theory of free trade as handed down by Adam Smith and David Ricardo—even if often taken out of context, misinterpreted, selectively chosen, and inappropriate for today's circumstances—has become so much part of contemporary capitalist folklore that it will always find its adherents. This is not to rail against the system, only to point out that free trade has deep roots. Along with private property rights and anti-government sentiments, the doctrines of free trade provide the ideological foundation for a free market economy, and on that basis alone, they are always guaranteed a featured role. As we saw, free trade has been a topic of heated debate in Canada for well over a century, and while it has sometimes been placed on the back burner of the political agenda, there will always be a sizable portion of the population, particularly among the elite, that supports it. Yet the stature of this idea will likely be down-graded, and eventually free trade will lose its momentum as the Big Idea. History shows that most Big Ideas come with an expiration date, and no doubt, free trade, too, has a limited shelf life. Its appeal will probably wane in the process of making room for another Big Idea or because it no longer meets the needs of the political and economic elite. But it will never be completely eradicated and may resurface any time.

How is it that a simple idea—such as free trade is good or the deficit is bad—can survive in today's information age? Aren't most people in Canada well educated and capable of forming their own opinions? The dominance of a Big Idea might have been easy to understand in the past, when the majority of the population was illiterate and knowledge was jealously guarded by a small elite. But today things are different. Surely such demagoguery, we reason, is a relic of the past and has no place in an open and democratic society. The reality, however, is otherwise, and unpopular ideas continue to be shunned, although this process is considerably subtler today than in the past.

The fact is that no one likes dissent, and most people and organizations go out of their way to avoid it. Institutions, for example, tend to hire candidates who are in general agreement with their overall objectives. In order to have a realistic chance of being hired by the World Bank, a candidate is well advised to subscribe to the tenets of the free market. Since the majority of candidates who apply to the World Bank are in the possession of a PhD, it is not difficult to ascertain which economic doctrines they subscribe to. A dissertation assailing the inequity of capitalist markets is not likely to result in a job offer. In that sense, the organization ensures that its ideological bias is perpetuated. By simply ignoring applicants who are at odds with its agenda, the World Bank guarantees conformity. This provincialism serves the institution well and precludes any kind of intellectual challenges from within. Similarly, the political and media elite rely on mechanisms that ensure opposing viewpoints are not given equal legitimacy. While outright repression is sometimes resorted to, as was the case when the RCMP pepper-sprayed demonstrators at the 1997 APEC (Asia Pacific Economic Cooperation) summit in Vancouver, such tactics are usually not worth the effort, as the subsequent inquiry showed. Violence is also hugely unpopular with the public and suggests totalitarianism, always a dangerous proposition. Most important, in the presence of a well-nurtured Big Idea, violence is completely gratuitous. The Big Idea, by sheer volume alone, effectively crowds out any dissenting opinion. An endless stream of glowing news reports, editorials, and political speeches, compounded by soporific repetition, combine to ensure that free trade is consistently presented in a positive light. And admittedly, a Big Idea does make life simpler. No need to make things complicated by raising bothersome questions and entertaining informed debates. And the less doubt there exists about the Big Idea, the simpler political life becomes. This approach has been used to great effect in Canada. In the mainstream media, dissenting views are given only minimal space, and when so, are often ridiculed. Protestors just do not understand, they are naive, twentieth-century Luddites, hypocrites, "biting the hands that feeds us" as a headline in *The Globe and Mail* put it.[83]

Different Interests

Adam Smith famously wrote that we, society as a collective, benefit from the self-interest of the butcher, the brewer, and the baker. This sentiment was updated in a speech by Gordon Gekko, a character in the movie *Wall Street*, who summarized the 1980s business ethos as "Greed is good." Free trade theory introduces a contradiction of this simple premise, for it asks all participants to put aside their self-interest when it comes to international trade. That is, the theory of free trade asserts that once individuals, businesses, and countries forget about their self-interest and trade freely among one another, everybody will benefit. In short, self-interest is good for individual societies, but not when it comes to international trade. Does that mean we need to devise a system that separates good greed from bad? Even if we were able to properly distinguish between the two, how would we channel that self-interest once it no longer served the common weal? How can we expect the butcher to suddenly ignore his self-interest, previously praised, when his business is threatened by foreign competitors? Should we expect him to passively accept the judgment of the market? Of course not, and even if we did, it is doubtful he would. What is true for individuals and small businesses goes for entire industries as well as countries. In a society organized around selfishness, it is naive to expect industries to voluntarily shed that self-interest when it comes to international matters. Since there is no definitive evidence to show that free trade does work, we must grow comfortable with the fact that there will always be opposition to it. Likewise, we must understand that governments are not going to ignore their constituents in the name of some abstract theory. Yet it is exactly this kind of behaviour that advocates of free trade expect.

In that sense, free trade theory falls apart because it glosses over the simple fact that society comprises diverse interests. And different interests often translate into conflict. A northern pipeline is likely to be supported by those who will profit from it, but opposed by those whose land it is designed to traverse. Oil companies and their shareholders benefit; Aboriginals do not. The doctrine of free trade attempts to circumvent this clash of interests by declaring that free trade is to the advantage of everybody. But centuries of political struggle show this to be patently false. Landowners have interests that differ from those of industrialists, which differ from those of workers; those in dominating export industries have interests that clash with those of less competitive industries. The service industry has different interests from manufacturing industries. To universally advocate free trade is to pretend that all these interests align at some point, which they never have and never will. A theory simply cannot wish away these conflicts. Different interests endure, and free trade, because it always benefits some industries at the expense of others, will never be universally accepted.

Self-interest does indeed play an important role here. As we have seen, in some instances even the most unusual suspects, including Bob Rae and Oxfam, advocate free trade when it happens to suit their purpose. And so it goes for much of the free trade saga, people are all for it as long as it benefits their cause. But when the tables are turned, and free trade is no longer in their best interest, politicians and industrialists are just as quick to clamour for protection. It is easy to find fault with the United States because it so often breaks the rules, but all countries would surely do the same given the opportunity. There are no priests among the countries of the world when it comes to free trade. Even countries that earnestly preach the advantages of free trade quickly abandon its principles when it fails to work in their favour. And this probably amounts to the biggest myth that underlies free trade: that all evidence to the contrary, countries can somehow be trained to be altruistic and work for the common good. The fact is that countries are self-interested actors, and are rarely concerned about the welfare of others. If that were the case, foreign aid would be up, and Africa would not be poor. We should therefore not be surprised when governments do everything in their power to undermine free trade, particularly if doing so will advance the national interest. After all, have we not been told for over two hundred years that self-interest is a positive attribute?

It is worthwhile noting that most of the rhetoric about fairness and free trade originates with the right. One need not be reminded that it is also the right that protests against the urge to legislate equality in the domestic sphere, arguing that the market itself is the best mechanism to decide such matters. If a worker fails to get a job, government neither need nor should interfere to correct that social ill. Yet when it comes to free trade, the right has found it difficult to adhere even to the simplest edict of laissez-faire, which is to leave it alone. The WTO and other trade institutions are precisely about legislating equality: that prohibition does not meet international standards, this subsidy is unfair, this tariff unjust. With trade agreements like the GATT and NAFTA, countries are now subject to more scrutiny than ever before, not only by international organizations but also by other countries suspicious of how they conduct their affairs. In the end, these institutions enforce rules to such a degree that free trade is anything but. Similar to a "free gift," the "free" in "free trade" should alert people to the fact that there is actually very little freedom involved.

In the public relations war over free trade, the right has also accused the left of running out of ideas. At the heart of this charge is that the left relies too much on the antiquated ideas of Keynesian-style intervention—to support fledgling industries, fund health care, educate the masses, ameliorate poverty. As evidence of the failure of these policies, detractors point to the economic slowdown of the 1970s, high inflation, and mounting deficits. In short, the right declares Keynesianism to be dead, and if not quite so, at least it should be. But its position on free trade demonstrates that the right is itself locked in a world that goes back not only decades, but centuries.

Similarly, the left has used the debate over free trade as an opportunity to air long-lasting grievances about the free market. Its most serious charge is that the WTO is autocratic and unresponsive to the will of the people, a world government without democratic representation. But this charge is difficult to uphold. The WTO is represented by its 144 member governments and, in that sense, is as representative of the will of the people as the average democratic government. Democracy, however, has never been a guarantor of perfect equality. Many people are critical of how the democratic process works even within countries, claiming that business has undue influence on political matters, that governments themselves are autocratic, and that many, particularly the poor, are disenfranchised. The debate about democracy is complex and beyond the scope of this book, but the point is that any charge made against the WTO can equally well be made against any democratic state.

In any case, corporations do not take part in the WTO negotiations; and neither do non-governmental organizations, such as environmental or human rights groups. Each member country gets one vote, no matter how big its population or how powerful in economic terms. Of course, this is in theory only, and in practice the amount of influence each group or country is able to wield varies dramatically, much the same way that not every citizen in Canada has equal influence over domestic policy. Big business plays a powerful role in the US trade agenda, whereas in France farmers continue to exert considerable influence. Power imbalances do exist, but this still makes it difficult to conclude, as some left wing commentators have, that the GATT is a Magna Carta for corporate capital or that the WTO constitutes a new world government.

Third World

Theories about laissez-faire and free trade are historically specific and should not be taken out of this context. Free trade might well have been beneficial to Great Britain when it was technologically, economically, and militarily so advanced that it had virtually no competitors. In the nineteenth century, there existed an almost unlimited market for manufactured goods, with only a handful of suppliers competing. In contrast, today there are few markets left unexplored and an excess of suppliers. In the current environment, it is exceedingly difficult for new producers to enter already established markets. While there may be opportunities for Third World competitors in the clothing and textiles industry, or even smaller manufactured goods, this cannot be said for the more lucrative high-tech sector. It is inconceivable that a Third World country like Indonesia could compete in the automobile or aerospace industry on the basis that these markets are already monopolized by Europe, North America, and Japan. The advantages the First World has been able to accumulate over the centuries provide it with a head start that makes it impossible for the Third World to catch up. A country that is technologically and economically backward, in addition to being bogged down by debt, cannot possibly hope to compete in the global economy in such unfavourable circumstances.

Again, this reveals that not all countries are equal. Third World countries simply do not have the resources, economically or culturally, to make their priorities heard. Accordingly, the First World in general—and the United States in particular—has been able to fashion trade rules to its own advantage. But even if free trade agreements were justly designed and enforced, the First World would continue to have the upper hand because of its technological and economic superiority. Which country is more likely to discover a cure for cancer, map out the remainder of the genome project, or design software that will drive a car: Vietnam or the United States, Uzbekistan or Japan, Brazil or Germany? The obvious answers illustrate that people intuitively know that the cards are stacked in favour of the First World. Poor countries do not even have a chance.

Last and not least, it makes no sense to allow countries to practise state intervention in their own economies but to forbid them to do so when it comes to international trade. The GATT allows welfare state subsidies within countries, but prohibits them for products traded on the international marketplace. In other words, Keynesianism is condoned on a national level but not an international one. This is particularly hypocritical with respect to poor countries. Western countries, through organizations like the World Bank and the IMF, force poor countries to practise laissez-faire, while they themselves spend half of their GDP on government services. In order to effectively compete in the global economy, poor countries are in need of considerable assistance from the First World. Not only should the First World allow poor countries to subsidize their industries, but it should actively assist them in doing so; and not with loans, but with grants and aid.

Imagine: A World without Trade Organizations

Few people would support the extreme alternative of having no trade at all. They are not opposed to trade *per se*, only to supranational institutions, and would like to see power revert to the national level. Anarchists, who play an important role in the fight against free trade, are particularly opposed to any kind of control from above. But since countries are self-interested actors, autonomy does not seem like a workable solution either. It is difficult to imagine how the world would function better without some sort of trade organization. Its absence would leave a power vacuum that would quickly be filled by the rich countries. This power advantage would allow them to do as they pleased, more so than even now. Some would argue, and rightfully so, that this would not be all that different from the status quo. We have seen plenty of evidence throughout this book that economic might translates directly into political power and the ability to gets one's way. With no bigger power to effectively police its trade policies, the United States is left with a relatively free rein over how it conducts itself in the international arena. It rails against Japanese import restrictions, but has no problems closing its own borders to Korean steel. Many countries have joined the WTO in the hope that it would act as an antidote to this blatant mishandling of power by the United States. The string of free trade agreements that Canada signed was motivated by exactly these concerns. As we saw, these developments are far from new, and for over 150 years Canada has pursued a deal with the United States in hope of taming the giant to the south. But even with a series of agreements in place, Canada has found it difficult to contain American protectionism. Still, this comes down to an important matter of degree, for with organizations like the WTO, countries have at least some recourse to justice. In this light, some kind of organization to oversee global trade is preferable to none at all.

The WTO is not likely to win any popularity contests soon, and some of the blame must lie with the institution itself. Part of the problem is that the WTO seems to have convinced itself that free trade can actually be accomplished. Just enough rules and regulations and eventually the world will function as a smoothly oiled trading machine. But the reality is otherwise, and individual countries will continue to challenge the WTO rules, to undermine them, and, if all else fails, to ignore them. Unfortunately for the WTO, and fortunately for those who oppose it, the WTO does not have the resources, either in terms of power or finances, to ensure that everybody abides by the rules. The trickery, deceit, and sleight of hand that have historically been used to protect domestic industries now just have a legal recourse. Countries examine each other's production and trade practices and, with almost religious zeal, are able to find fault. Europe is planning to take the United States to the WTO for unfair tax structure; the United States is convinced that low stumpage fees in British Columbia amount to nothing more than a subsidy. The only thing that the WTO has been able to accomplish, it seems, is to globalize an American style of litigation.

Another reason why the WTO has not received the respect it feels it deserves is that it has bitten off more than it can chew. Intellectual property rights, services, and investors' rights, to say nothing of issues like food safety and the environment, can only be an indication of overzealousness and obsession. Particularly given its dearth of financial and human resources, the WTO might be well advised to focus its energies on some of the more contentious issues involving trade in goods before moving on to other sectors of the economy. Trade in goods may be a lot less glamorous, but it is nevertheless important. If the WTO were to deal properly with agriculture and textiles, and for the time being ignore issues such as intellectual property and investors' rights, it would go a long way in backing its claim that free trade benefits poor countries. Currently, critics accuse the WTO of tackling issues that primarily benefit the already wealthy countries. Going after services only makes this charge stick. In any case, the WTO does not have the resources to effectively deal with all these issues, which only serves to further undermine its credibility. By focusing on only a few select issues and working towards plausible solutions, the WTO could greatly enhance its reputation and at the same time bolster its public image.

I am going to end this book with an analogy that demonstrates how difficult it is to force one's wishes on society. Although obviously disparate topics, both abortion and trade are illustrative of the conflict that often exists between values and action. Free trade, it is generally agreed upon, is a positive thing, but is impossible to enforce because countries are self-interested actors and consequently will always intervene in their economies. Abortion has been equally difficult to legislate; even when illegal, those who want an abortion will usually find a way. Yet there is always a segment in society that wants to proscribe this activity. As we know, social conservatives are particularly keen on prohibiting abortions, not only for themselves, but for everybody. More liberal individuals tend to lean towards the opinion that if somebody chooses to have an abortion, it is her decision to make. But liberals also realize that they should not be able to force this preference on others. Despite such differences of opinion, biologically speaking, conservatives and liberals are remarkably similar and equally likely, despite best intentions, to get pregnant. An unplanned pregnancy is seldom welcome, but it puts conservatives in a particularly awkward position. Since conservatives also preach abstinence, a pregnancy is testament to misbehaviour. In order to save face, they often feel compelled to have an abortion.[84] Even conservative politicians who support anti-abortion legislation have publicly admitted that if their daughter or sister were to become pregnant, the decision to have an abortion would ultimately be hers.

The similarity between abortion and free trade lies in the fact that a sizable chasm separates people's convictions, often strongly held, and subsequent behaviour. Politicians may wax eloquent about how this (free trade) or that (no abortion) would make the world a better place, but such a world is simply not attainable. Once more practical issues arise (Do we really want everyone to see that our fourteen-year-old daughter is pregnant?), people will go through all sorts of ideological contortions to justify an abortion. Ditto with trade: Once a local industry is threatened with extinction, even the most ardent free trader will go to considerable lengths to save it, including the application of subsidies and tariffs (precisely the programs that are illegal under free trade). For whatever reason, many a naive politician believes—usually when things are going his way—that his support for whatever cause is genuine, unyielding, morally superior, and impossible to compromise. But this quickly changes once politicians are confronted with more practical matters. In other words, it is impossible to legislate some behaviour, and if a government decides to do so anyway, people will find all kinds of ways to get around it. Free trade is an issue that finds itself in this netherworld, and this fact alone should put at ease people who are concerned about the evils of free trade. Too many competing and contradictory interests guarantee that it will never happen.

Still, Canada continues to actively pursue more free trade agreements. Despite tepid results—the income of Canadians relative to other countries has fallen, and productivity has stagnated throughout the 1990s—our government has decided that free trade is the route that will lead us to economic prosperity.[85] Yet, as we have seen, the seemingly simple relationship between trade and growth is remarkably difficult to demonstrate. While the consequences of free trade have been negligible for Canada and the First World in general, the same cannot be said for the Third. In poor countries, the repercussions of forced trade likely include a rise in poverty, at least in relative terms. In other words, the consequences of free trade range from neutral in Canada (at best) to demonstrably negative in the Third World. Such results hardly spell success and suggest it is time for a change.

Notes

Introduction

1. The first survey specifically asked about the Canada US Free Trade Agreement and included only Canada and the United States. Later surveys ask about the North American Free Trade Agreement (NAFTA; see Glossary).

2. See Linda McQuaig. *Shooting the Hippo*. Toronto: Penguin Books, 1995. Also, Jim Standford. *The Paper Boom*. Ottawa: Canadian Centre for Policy Alternatives, 1999.

1 Free Trade: Theory and Practice

3. "Blair's Rare Address to Canadian MPs Pushes Free Trade," *Vancouver Sun*, February 23, 2001, A5.

4. "Speaking Out for Trade," *The Globe and Mail*, February 24, 2001, A12.

5. Gordon Ritchie. *Wrestling with the Elephant*. Toronto: MacFarlane Walter & Ross, 1997, 20.

6. Michael Hart. *Fifty Years of Canadian Tradecraft*. Ottawa: Centre for Trade and Law, 1998, 18.

7. Sidney Weintraub. *NAFTA at Three: A Progress Report*. Washington, DC: Center for Strategic & International Studies, 1997.

8. Graham Dunkley. *The Free Trade Adventure* (2nd ed). New York: Zed Books, 2000.

9. Brian Mulroney. "What's in Free Trade for Canada?" *The Globe and Mail*. April 17, 2001, A15.

10. John Herd Thompson with Allen Seager. *Canada 1922–1939, Decades of Discord*. Toronto: McClelland and Stewart, 1985.

11. Paul Krugman. *Peddling Prosperity*. New York: W.W. Norton & Company, 1994, 25.

12. Graham Dunkley, *Free Trade Adventure*, 23.

13. Paul Krugman. *The Age of Diminished Expectations* (2nd ed). Cambridge, MA: MIT Press, 1994.

14. Patricia Marchak. *The Integrated Circus*. Montreal: McGill-Queens University Press, 1991, 46.

2 Adam Smith: The Free Market Revealed

15. Those familiar with pre-twentieth-century economics are aware that writers preferred the phrase "political economy," as they recognized that the two—political and economic power—are intimately linked. It was not until the twentieth century and the increased specialization that befell academia that the two separated into distinct disciplines: politics (political science) and economics. Although the division of labour can, as Smith puts forward, bring about many riches, some academics have lamented the separation of the two disciplines. Arguments that one cannot properly understand political power removed from the context of economic control account for a resurgence of political economy around the world in the past couple of decades, Canada included.

16. Adam Smith. *The Wealth of Nations*. Books 1–5. http://www.soc sci.mcmaster.ca/~econ/ugcm/3ll3/smith/wealth/

17. Karl Marx and Friedrich Engels. *Manifesto of the Communist Party*. Moscow: Progress Publishers, 1986, 36.

18. Smith, unlike Marx, did not advocate that the state should be wholly dismantled and felt it had an important role to play in terms of military defence and funding programs like education.

19. It will probably come as a surprise to many that Canada's trade is now less than one-quarter (about 22 percent) transcontinental. Almost

four-fifths (78 percent) of Canadian trade is with Canada's closest and only contiguous neighbour, the United States.

20. Adam Smith, *The Wealth*, Book 1, Chapter 7.

21. Ibid, Book 1, Chapter 10.

22. Ibid, Book 1, Chapter 11, Conclusion.

23. Marx and Engels, *Manifesto of the Communist Party*.

24. P. F. Speed. *Social Problems of the Industrial Revolution*. Wheaton and Company, 1975. The data do not specify whether the average age of death differed between the sexes, a not-insubstantial point.

25. Ibid, 51.

26. These laws have some interesting vestiges in Canada. The federal government of Canada, under the now-abolished Canada Assistance Plan (CAP), guaranteed to pay 50 percent of a province's social assistance expenditures as long as there were no residence requirements. That meant that someone who moved from Alberta to Ontario could collect benefits as soon as she arrived. BC premier Mike Harcourt challenged this stipulation when he imposed a three-month residency requirement after the federal government unilaterally made cuts to the CAP.

27. Marx and Engels, *Manifesto of the Communist Party*, 36.

3 David Ricardo: So What Does That Have to Do with the Price of Corn in England?

28. Although the steam engine was already in use in Smith's time, its full potential had not been exploited yet. It was invented as early as the end of the seventeenth century, and greatly improved upon by James Watt in 1769. Its application, however, remained limited for decades (it was initially used to pump water out of mine shafts). It took years of tinkering before the steam engine was incorporated into industrial production (for example, textiles) and transportation (railway and steamships).

29. Robert Heilbroner. *The Worldly Philosophers*. New York: Touchstone, 1980, 78–79.

30. Mark Blaug. *David Ricardo* (1772–1823). Brookfield, VT: Elgar Publishing, 1991, xi.

31. Herman Daly and John Cobb. *For the Common Good* (2nd ed). Boston: Beacon Press, 1994, 209. This is also a good source to consult for a detailed discussion of comparative advantage, 209–35.

32. This point is usually illustrated by way of analogy, the following being a typical example. An introductory textbook entitled *Economics* (Ake Blomqvist, Paul Wonnacott, and Ronald Wonnacott [3rd ed]. Toronto: McGraw Hill Ryerson Limited, 1990, 47.) uses the example of a lawyer and a gardener who are faced with the need to divide a number of tasks. The lawyer has an absolute advantage in both gardening and knowledge of the law, but she is best advised to spend her time doing legal work since it is more lucrative. Although this analogy seems to add some understanding to the issue, it is also, unfortunately, wrong-headed in that it omits some important details. In order for this to be an accurate analogy, both workers would have to be trained in both legal work and gardening, as both Portugal and England are capable of producing wine and cloth. In this sense, individuals and countries differ in important ways, and consequently this kind of analogy quickly crumbles. Countries comprise a multitude of people who have a multitude of skills, whereas workers usually have only a limited number of skills.

33. I say relative because, first, it is difficult to measure success in an era before GDP was used, and, second, to then trace the outcome to one single factor such as free trade would be disingenuous.

34. Tim Armstrong, a long-time trade bureaucrat, makes the argument that Canada should subsidize its automobile industry more, for this is exactly what the United States is doing. "Industry Loves a Good Carrot," *The Globe and Mail*, May 29, 2002, A17.

35. Greg Keenan. "Ford Warns: Subsidize or Lose Jobs," *The Globe and Mail*, November 9, 2002.

4 John Maynard Keynes: Challenging the Classical Economists

36. The actual quote is *"laissez faire* was planned." Karl Polanyi. *The Great Transformation.* Boston: Beacon Press, 1957, 141.

37. In light of these criticisms, it is worthwhile noting that the Allied powers did not repeat the same mistake following the Second World War and channelled billions of dollars into Germany to prop up its near-non-existant economy.

38. Robert Heilbroner, *Worldly Philosophers,* 249.

39. This quote is actually from *A Tract on Monetary Reform.* London: Macmillan and Co., 1923.

5 The History of Free Trade in Canada

40. In the interest of detail, Columbus never did land on the continent itself, but only on a series of Caribbean islands, including Hispaniola (which he first thought was Japan). He did eventually sight Venezuela, which is now part of the South American continent, but never set foot on it.

41. Glen Norcliffe. "Foreign Trade in Goods and Services," *Canada in the Global Economy* (ed. J. Britton). Montreal: McGill-Queen's University Press, 1996, 25.

42. Kenneth Norrie and Douglas Owram. *A History of the Canadian Economy.* Toronto: Harcourt Brace Canada, 1996, 177.

43. Randall White. *Fur Trade to Free Trade* (2nd ed). Toronto: Dundurn Press, 1989.

44. Angus Maddison. *Monitoring the World Economy, 1820 to 1992.* Paris: OECD, 1995, 61.

6 *World Trade: The* GATT *and the* WTO

45. From www.craigmarlatt.com/craig/canada/government/turner.html, accessed October 5, 2001.

46. Each country, including Australia, New Zealand, and South Africa, signed separate trade deals with each of the other countries. This is in contrast to multilateral trade agreements, such as NAFTA and the GATT, in which each country treats all other members the same. In the lingo of trade agreements: without discrimination.

47. Michael Hart, *Trade Craft*, 41.

48. Graham Dunkley, *Free Trade Adventure*, 27.

49. Linda McQuaig. *The Quick and the Dead*. Toronto: Penguin Books, 1992, 3–4.

50. GM alone pays out US $3.9 billion a year in health insurance for 1.25 million people (including workers, their dependants, and retirees). The study was conducted by the American investment firm Morgan Stanley Dean Witter & Co. *The Globe and Mail*, February 12, 2002, B10.

51. Greg Keenan. "Overseas Makers Target Good Ol' Boys' Pickups," *The Globe and Mail*, June 25, 2002, B1 and B7.

52. Barrie McKenna. "The Road to Doha Is Fraught with US Trade Barriers," *The Globe and Mail*, November 9, 2001, B8.

53. Bruce Little. "Domestic Politics Skews US View of Fair Trade," *The Globe and Mail*, March 28, 2002, B15.

54. William Thorsell. "Second Thoughts on Free Trade," *The Globe and Mail*, May 14, 2001, A13.

55. Dalton Camp. "First Casualty of the Summit Should Be Propaganda," *The Toronto Star*, April 22, 2001, A13.

56. This is not to say that power in the WTO is equally dispersed among member countries. Although the organization is democratic, at least on the surface, poorer countries are unable to fully participate because they cannot always afford to send delegates to meetings. As well, smaller countries do not have the resources, either financial or

cultural, to take cases to court. Smaller countries also have less input in setting the agenda than do their wealthier counterparts. Observers critical of the institution note that no decision gets ratified unless consented to by the quadrilateral countries: the United States, the European Union, Japan, and Canada.

57. Everett Hughes. "Good People and Dirty Work," *The Pleasures of Sociology* (ed. Lewis Coser). Scarborough, ON: Mentor, 1980, 472–84.

7 Case Studies: Trade, the Environment, and National Sovereignty

58. Jimmy Carter. "A Flawed Timber Market," *The New York Times*, March 24, 2001, A13.

59. Methylcyclopentadienyl Manganese Tricarbonyl.

60. *The American Journal of International Law*, 94, 2000, 159–60.

61. Neville Nankivell. "Much Is Confusing About MMT Bill," *Financial Post Daily*, March 6, 1997, 15.

62. John Geddes. "Ethyl Corp to Fight Potential MMT Ban," *The Financial Post*, November 21, 1995, 8.

63. Ken Traynor. "MMT Fuel Additive Scandal: The Fiasco Represents Jean Chrétien's Free Trade Chickens Coming Home to Roost," *Briarpatch* 27 (7), Summer 1998, 7–10.

64. Geoff Winestock. "Poor Countries Lose Out Under EU's Trade Agenda," *The Globe and Mail*, Wednesday, August 8, 2001, B7.

8 Free Trade and the Third World

65. This should give pause to those who think that there are no alternatives. Had Sweden, France, or the Soviet Union designed the post-war architecture, we would surely be living in a different world today.

66. There are three additional institutions associated with the World Bank, but these are not usually included under the rubric of the World Bank. They are the International Finance Corporation (IFC), the Multilateral Investment Guarantee Agency (MIGA), and the International Center for Settlement of Investment Disputes (ICSID).

67. The factual information about the World Bank is from its Web site, as well as from Susan George and Fabrizio Sabelli. *Faith and Credit: The World Bank's Secular Empire*. Toronto: Penguin Books, 1994.

68. Absolute poverty is usually measured in terms of caloric intake and life expectancy.

69. Susan George and Fabrizio Sabelli, *Faith and Credit*, 18–19.

70. Partly for that reason, it is quite difficult to get accurate and intelligible information about the IMF. One of the best sources that I have come across is *Arming NGOs with Knowledge: A Guide to the International Monetary Fund*, available at http://www.foe.org/international/imf/handbook.pdf

71. Marcus Gee. "In Praise of Sweatshops," *The Globe and Mail*, April 19, 2000, A17.

72. Angus Maddison, *Monitoring the World Economy*.

73. Adam Smith, *The Wealth*.

74. Greg Palast. BBC transcripts, Friday, April 27, 2001. Interview with Joseph Stiglitz. http://gregpalast.com/detail.cfm?artid=97&row=1

75. These data are from *The Economist*, March 23, 2000, but were originally collected by the OECD. The OECD stands for the Organisation for Economic Co-operation and Development, and is a statistics-gathering organization and think-tank for the thirty richest countries in the world. People may be familiar with it because it secretly attempted to pass the Multilateral Agreement on Investment (MAI) in the late 1990s. The pact was exposed by the Council of Canadians and talks collapsed shortly afterward.

76. The figure for the United States will probably increase in the near future, as the American government introduced the US $100 billion farm bill in 2002.

77. "A Not-So-Perfect Market," *The Economist*, March 23, 2000, 8–10.

9 Production, Consumption, and Employment: Will the Circle Be Unbroken?

78. "Bush's Trade Policy: All Talk, No Action" *The Globe and Mail*, June 8, 2001, A12.

79. Adam Smith, *The Wealth*, Book 4, Chapter 8.

80. Some economists argue that a recession is a good thing on the basis that more competitive industries are able to pick up capital goods at bargain prices. Aristotle Onassis built his shipping fleet during the Depression in just such a way.

81. Gordon Ritchie, *Wrestling with the Elephant*, 22.

82. During the course of writing this book I was struck by how the mere mention of government assistance provoked a negative reaction in me, showing how well I had been socialized into the free trade dogma. At some point I was able to break free of this ideology and realized that this was just a prejudice with no basis in fact. Not only do governments interfere in the economy all the time, it is often the better for it.

Conclusion: The Future of Free Trade

83. Alan Rugman and Karl Moore. "Biting the Hand that Feeds Us," *The Globe and Mail*, January 4, 2002, A13.

84. This is backed by research in the United States that shows that conservatives are just as likely to have abortions as liberals. Samuel and Cynthia Janus. *The Janus Report on Sexual Behavior*. Toronto: Wiley and Sons, 1993.

85. Some people have made the argument that although things are bad, they would be even worse without free trade. This is like a pharmaceutical firm claiming, after extensive testing showing a drug to be ineffective, that without it the patient might be sicker still.

Glossary

Agreement on Trade-Related Aspects of Intellectual Property Rights (TRIPS): Agreement that oversees patents and copyrights under the World Trade Organization (WTO).

Agreement on Trade-Related Investment Measures (TRIMS): Agreement that oversees foreign investment under the World Trade Organization (WTO).

Asia Pacific Economic Cooperation (APEC): An association established in 1989, APEC is not a binding agreement. APEC seeks to promote trade among its twenty-one members located in Asia and North America (including Canada).

Business Council on National Issues (BCNI): Canadian business lobby representing 150 of the biggest corporations in Canada, including Bombardier Inc, General Motors of Canada, and the Royal Bank of Canada. Founded in 1976. Thomas d'Aquino is current president and chief executive. Recently underwent name change to Canadian Council of Chief Executives (2002).

Canadian Council of Chief Executives (CCCE): New name of Business Council on National Issues (BCNI) as of 2002 (see entry directly above).

Canada US Free Trade Agreement (FTA): Free trade agreement between Canada and United States, which became effective on January 1, 1989; replaced by NAFTA (North American Free Trade Agreement) on January 1, 1994.

Codex Alimentarius Commission (Codex): Organization located in Rome that oversees health standards for food; these standards have subsequently been adopted by the World Trade Organization (WTO). Founded in 1963 by the Food and Agriculture Organization (FAO) and

World Health Organization (WHO), both of which are specialized agencies of the United Nations (UN).

Common Agricultural Policy (CAP): Policy of the European Union (EU), which protects and regulates its agricultural industries, including the use of generous subsidies. Introduced in 1962.

Comparative Advantage: Theory of trade formulated in the mid-1800s that continues to provide the rationale for most modern trade agreements. Simply put, it states that all countries benefit if they trade freely among one another and specialize in whatever they are comparatively good at.

Corn Laws: A series of laws in Great Britain, introduced in 1436, which protected domestic farmers by regulating the importation of corn (British term for grain) through tariffs. The repeal of these laws in 1846 introduced free trade to Great Britain.

Countervailing Duties: Retaliatory duties placed on imports that are subsidized. These are legal under the General Agreement on Tariffs and Trade (GATT) if the country applying them can prove that the offending country is engaging in illegal practices.

Dumping: When a firm sells a product in a foreign market for less than its cost or less than its domestic price. This kind of activity is mostly engaged in to gain market share.

European Union (EU): European free trade zone comprising fifteen countries. Established in 1993, it replaced the European Community (EC; 1967), which in turn can be traced to the European Coal and Steel Community (1952). The latter was founded after the Second World War in order to foster trade and economic co-operation among European countries.

Foreign Direct Investment (FDI): Direct investment in industries or real estate in contrast to stocks or bonds (usually referred to as portfolio investment).

Free Trade Agreement of the Americas (FTAA): Proposed extension of the North American Free Trade Agreement (NAFTA). The FTAA is projected to eventually include all of North and South America.

General Agreement on Tariffs and Trade (GATT): Oldest and most important agreement under the World Trade Organization (WTO), which has overseen the trade of goods among its members since 1947.

General Agreement on Trade in Services (GATS): Agreement under the World Trade Organization (WTO) that oversees trade in services.

Gross Domestic Product (GDP): The total of goods and services produced in a country in a given time period, usually a year.

Gross World Product (GWP): The total of the combined gross domestic products of the earth's countries.

Hyperinflation: Very rapid inflation throughout a short time period. Although there is no agreed-upon threshold that distinguishes this type of inflation from the more normal variety, often called creeping inflation, anything over 1000 percent per annum can safely be considered hyperinflation. Ukraine, for example, experienced inflation of 5000 percent in 1993.

International Bank for Reconstruction and Development (IBRD): See World Bank.

International Development Association (IDA): See World Bank.

International Monetary Fund (IMF): Specialized agency of the United Nations (UN) that lends emergency funds to countries experiencing currency or balance of payment problems. Founded in 1944 at the Bretton Woods negotiations in New Hampshire. Headquartered in Washington, DC.

International Trade Organization (ITO): Planned forerunner of the World Trade Organization (WTO), but failed to be ratified in the late 1940s.

Keynesianism: Economic policy that advocates monetary and fiscal policies to keep employment and consumption high. Practised to some degree by all Western economies since the Second World War.

Mercantilism: An economic doctrine in which the state oversees all aspects of trade. Practised in the eighteenth and nineteenth centuries by the colonial powers of Europe. This usuallⁿ involved importing raw materials to the mother country and exporting manufactured products to the colonies.

Modernization Theory: A theory of development popular in the 1950s and 1960s. It projected that the poor countries of the world would eventually go through industrialization and become wealthy.

Most Favoured Nation (MFN): Non-discrimination clause under the GATT that requires members to treat all other members equally.

Multilateral Agreement on Investment (MAI): Investment agreement proposed by the Organisation for Economic Co-operation and Development (OECD). It was withdrawn because of widespread opposition in the late 1990s.

Non-Tariff Barrier (NTB): As the name suggests, a trade barrier that is not a tariff. Includes such tactics as unjustified technical or environmental prohibitions, as well as enforced quotas. Illegal under the World Trade Organization (WTO).

North American Free Trade Agreement (NAFTA): A free trade agreement among Canada, the United States, and Mexico. Took place of Canada US Free Trade Agreement in 1994.

Organization for Economic Cooperation and Development (OECD): Statistics-gathering organization, primarily for the wealthy countries; located in Paris. Launched in 1961, when it replaced the Organization for European Economic Cooperation (1948). Canada is one of its thirty members.

Precautionary, or Cautionary, Principle: States that if risks associated with a product, whether a pesticide, additive, or chemical substance, are not known, it should not be used. Difficult to implement, because without scientific evidence, the establishment of risk can be arbitrary and subjective.

Protectionism: The opposite of free trade, whereby countries protect domestic industry by keeping foreign products out through the use of tariffs or other trade barriers.

Reciprocity Treaty: Erstwhile term for free trade agreement.

Smoot Hawley Tariff: Trade bill introduced by American Congress in 1930 and named after Representative Willis C. Hawley and Senator Reed Smoot, both Republicans.

Structural Adjustment Programs (SAP): Programs associated with the World Bank and the International Monetary Fund (IMF). Also known as austerity programs. Imposition of strict monetary and fiscal programs that are attached to loans.

Transparency: Used in a variety of ways to mean without deceit, or free and open. For example, the World Trade Organization (WTO) stipulates that countries must not engage in trade barriers that are disguised as environmental standards. Trade barriers must be transparent; that is, readily apparent.

TRIMS: See Agreement on Trade-Related Investment Measures.

TRIPS: See Agreement on Trade-Related Aspects of Intellectual Property Rights.

Voluntary Export Restraint (VER): An agreement between two countries that limits the number of exports going from one country to another. Sometimes referred to as an export restraint, a VER is a clear protectionist measure and illegal under the World Trade Organization (WTO).

World Bank: In fact, two organizations: the International Bank for Reconstruction and Development (IBRD) and the International Development Association (IDA). Both are specialized agencies of the United Nations (UN). The IBRD was founded in 1944 at the Bretton Woods negotiations in New Hampshire and the IDA in 1960. The World Bank is headquartered in Washington, DC, with offices around the world.

World Trade Organization (WTO): Specialized agency of the United Nations (UN) located in Geneva. Founded in 1995 and overseer of thirty different agreements, including the General Agreement on Tariffs and Trade (GATT) and the General Agreement on Trade in Services (GATS).

Index